Altered Book Basics

Choosing a Book

When I choose a book, I tend to do so for a couple of reasons. The first is the price. I do not pay full price for a book at a bookstore unless I want to read it first. Mainly, because I'm cheap and I would rather spend the rest of my money on cool supplies, etc. Here is a list of places where I have found inexpensive books:
• Your local library may sell old hardback books
• Bargain bins in any bookstore
• Garage sales
• Half Price Books which sells books by the yard
• Thrift stores.

I look for catchy titles. Sometimes I like to theme a book around the title. Great book covers intrigue me. Older books with tooled leather covers are a real find. Be sure to look underneath book jackets. The size or shape book could be a deciding factor. I avoid paperbacks, magazines and book club books. Their bindings can break down quickly. If a binding does break down, you can always rebind it or go to a printing shop and have them coil bind the book.

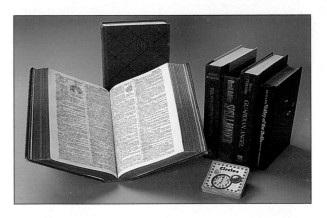

The Best Glues

Everyone has a favorite glue. I use Perfect Paper Adhesive™, matte medium, gel medium or a glue stick. I apply a very thin film to the page. I let pages dry before gluing more than one. (Tip: the starch content in paste glues may make them non-archival, the glues may attract bugs.)

The Structure of Your Book

How many pages are you going to alter? Do you want the book to lie flat? Is it a round robin or will you alter the whole book yourself? I rarely plan the structure of a whole book at the onset unless it is a short book or a children's book.

When working with a limited number of pages, it is important to have a plan. It's not that important when you have 300 pages to play with. Structure also has to do with the physical altering of the page. You can rip, burn, cut, sew, fold or glue a page to alter its structure. Think of it as the bones of your book. After you have the structure you want, it's time for the aesthetics.

Tip - Spread glue evenly over pages with stiff cardboard or a credit card.

Smooth glue between pages, working out from the center to remove air bubbles.

Tip - Paint Gesso over the cover and/or over pages to cover up unwanted words.

Gluing Pages Without Wrinkles

Probably the most asked question about altered books is *"How do you glue pages together without wrinkling them?"* There are many ways, but the most important thing is to understand what makes a paper page wrinkle.

Paper wrinkles because moisture is absorbed and makes one side of the paper shrink. When you apply an even amount of moisture to the other side, paper will flatten. If you use products with little moisture, the problem disappears. Here are some glues that give good results.

• **Perfect Paper Adhesive™ -** Apply matte (non glossy) adhesive as for gel medium. • **Gel Medium -** Apply a thin coat with a credit card. Press the next page down and smooth it with a clean card to push out any air bubbles.
• **Matte Medium** can wrinkle paper when applied to raw pages. Apply as for gel medium, place wax paper between the pages, let it sit with several books on top overnight.
• **Glue Stick -** Apply and then smooth out air bubbles.

Attach Pages -
Use Glue, Wire or Screws

Glue the Edges
by Beth Cote

It is easy to glue pages together. Glue goes on smooth and keeps pages flat. I like a good glue stick.

or Wire Pages Together
by Cindy Pestka

I find that wiring a 'block' (large group or stack) of pages together is a lot faster and easier than gluing.

1. Mark positions for holes on all pages (use a template if desired).

2. Punch holes with a hole puncher, a large pin or a small awl tool.

3. Thread wire through the holes. Cut a shadowbox hole.

4. Glue 'block' (stack of wired pages) to the back of the book.

To attach pages together with wire, use an awl, hole punch or drill to make 2 sets of small holes about 1" apart in the upper and lower corner of all the pages except the top page. Place a small piece of wood behind the last page so you don't drill into the cover. Cut two 6" pieces of thin wire or heavy thread.

Starting at the top right corner, loop wire or thread up through one hole and down through the other. Twist or tie the loose ends together on the back to secure the pages. Don't pull too tight or the pages will buckle. Position the twist or knot under the last page so it is out of sight. Repeat for the remaining corner.

Add final embellishments such as ribbon or tulle behind the top page before finishing and before gluing down the top page. Cut out tulle just smaller than size of page. Attach the tulle between first and second pages on all 4 sides using White glue or permanent paper adhesive. Press down firmly.

Or experiment with running a strip of ribbon, a strand of beads or a strand of pearls across the window. Glue in place and apply White glue, permanent paper adhesive or hot glue on all 4 sides to glue down the top page. Press down firmly.

To make a shadowbox, open the book and clip the page or pages which are to be the front of your shadowbox to the front cover of the book. Clip the back page or pages to the back cover. All the rest of the pages are the 'block' (or large group).

You need small clamps or very large 'bulldog' clips.

Move the clamps around while gluing to make sure all areas are covered. Let dry overnight.

Remove clamps and cut a shadowbox into the 'block' of pages with a craft knife. Use a template or metal edge ruler. As you cut deeper and remove the inside, the edges will be a guide. **TIP:** Save the pages for collages on other projects. When you are finished carefully cut the opening in front page a little smaller than the opening in 'block'. Alter page and glue it on front of 'block'. Finish back page as desired, glue it to 'block'. **NOTE:** Sometimes you need extra strength in the back and gluing several pages together or gluing the back cover to the 'block' is ideal. You can also divide a book into halves and proceed as above using 2 'blocks' with one 'block' glued to each cover for a double shadowbox effect.

or Screw the Book Shut

Sometimes screws are the easiest and most secure method.

Drill holes in pages and screw together.

This technique uses screws instead of glue to hold the 'block' shut. Be sure to leave at least 2 pages at the front and back to cover the screw heads when finished. Open book and clip front pages to front cover. Clip back pages to back cover.

Remaining pages are the 'block'. Use small screws equal in length to depth of book and an electric drill. Place a screw in each corner of 'block'. Cut shadowbox with a craft knife.

When you begin, use a template or metal edge ruler. As you cut deeper and remove inside paper, paper edges can be your guide. When you are finished, carefully cut opening in front pages a little smaller than the opening in 'block'.

Alter pages then glue on 'block'. Finish back page then glue it to 'block'.

Embellish Your Altered Book

Collage Color Papers

- **Look for collage elements** in books, make color photocopies of vintage photographs, computer generate text or use scraps of art paper, wallpaper, wrapping paper, magazines, calendars, catalogs, stickers, postcards, tissue paper and paper napkins.
- **Choose a selection** of collage elements by theme and/or by color.
- **Experiment with placement** of collage elements. Use a small piece of double-stick tape to hold papers while determining placement.
- **Once you are pleased** with the design, use White glue to add collage elements inside and outside book.
- **Antique papers** before or after gluing if desired.

Collage Clips

- **Collect black and white drawings**, illustrations, old certificates, lettering and favorite words.
- **Photocopy** the items in black and white or use the original pieces.
- **'Age' the black and white elements** following the basic instructions on pages 22-23.
- **Tint elements** or add colors and highlights with colored pencils, chalks and inks.
- **Add color washes** with Fluid gels and acrylics following the basic instructions on pages 26-27.
- **A few Collage Clips,** drawings and words are included on pages 44-47 to get you started. It is easy to copy these on a black and white copier.

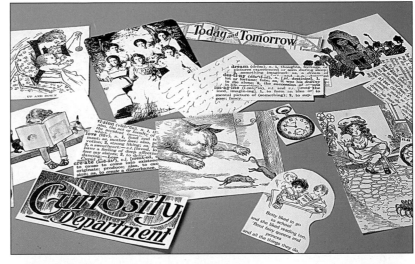

Trinkets & Treasures

- **Use tags, beads, fibers,** foreign coins, tassels, old keys, dried or silk flowers, skeleton leaves, glass bottles, marbles, game tiles, buttons, charms, puzzle pieces, mica tiles, jewelry, playing cards, feathers, small picture frames, ribbons, polymer or paper clay pieces, seashells, mosaic tiles, envelopes, fabric swatches, chess pieces, upholstery braid, press-on letters, bottle corks, rhinestones, wire, twigs, typewriter keys, rulers, beach glass, hardware, little metal tins, compass, lace, fibers.
- **Once you are happy with the design,** use White glue or hot glue for lighter pieces and a strong adhesive like E-6000 for large, heavy or glass embellishments... design is limited only by your imagination!
- **Tips:** Try using old magazines and catalogs when gluing. Place your paper on a clean page, apply glue to the back using a foam brush then turn the page for a clean work surface.
- **Use an awl** or drill to make a hole through the front cover or spine. Thread various fibers through, knotting loosely on each side of the hole. Add beads, charms or stamped tags as desired.

Imagine
by Nancy Curry

MATERIALS: Book • Medium weight vellum • Rubber stamps (message, 2 backgrounds) • Champagne Metallic ink • Black Brilliance ink • Halo Violet/Gold Lumiere paint • Seed beads • Copper metallic floss • Perfect Paper adhesive • Matte sealer • Gel medium • .5 Micron pen • Sponge • Cutting mat • Craft knife • Heat gun

TIPS: Press metallic ink pad randomly around page to stain. Stamp swirled lines vertically with Champagne ink and Lumiere paint. Reverse stamp intermittently to create an interesting pattern. Add random markings with side of sponge. Seal with matte sealer. Cut wavy window. Cut 5" square of vellum into vertical freeform strips stopping 1/2" from top and bottom edges. Cut another 5" square of vellum into thin strips and weave strips into first. Weave floss and beads with beading needle. Secure beads with paper adhesive. Attach weaving between windows with glue or tape. Write quote under window. Apply Lumiere paint to page and facing page. Let dry. Stamp message on vellum with Black ink. Heat set. Center vellum vertically behind window and attach. Using same Lumiere paint, apply texture stamp to book pages and over vellum. Seal pages with matte sealer to prevent sticking.

When looking for a book to alter, don't overlook books that have holes already cut into them. It's fun and interesting to use books that have a structure in place when you buy them.

Helpful Hint

While punches make an easy window, you can cut unusual shapes with a craft knife and a cutting mat. If you are going to sandwich an item between 2 pages be sure to cut through both pages at the same time.

How to Cut Holes, Windows, Niches & Deep Shadowboxes
by Beth Cote

Niches do not have to be full of three dimensional items. The subtle simplicity of the pages can be enhanced by bright colors surrounding the niche contrasted with simple photographs or drawings.

An easy way to add visual interest is to cut away a bit of a page. There is something wonderful about being able to see just a tantalizing bit of the next page. A window is a special technique used frequently in altered books. It gives the viewer a glimpse of the next page or a glimpse into a pocket whispering a clue of what might be inside. When you plan a window, consider what the reader will see. If you want the viewer to see the next page, consider the option of gluing 2 pages together for extra strength.

Some things to keep in mind when you cut into your book: Know why you're cutting. Cutting a window or a few pages involves different techniques than gutting a book. Have a plan in mind, so you can use the system that will work best. • Examine the pages. Old books can have very brittle pages. Be sure to have cardboard under the last page you are cutting and do not press or drag too hard. Bend a page to examine the brittleness.

I have bent a page and had it break in my hand. Not all old books are brittle, examine the one you're thinking of altering. • New books tend to be a bit stiffer. Glossy pages can be slick, so be careful and use a metal ruler with a cork backing instead of a template. • Book boards need to be cut one page at a time and require several runs with a craft knife to go through one page. Once the first page is finished, you can use that for a template.

When you cut a window, place matboard or a cutting mat under the last page. If you plan to have the windows sandwich an item, be sure to cut both windows at the same time for a good fit. **TIP:** I love using punches for windows. You can get an almost perfect circle with a punch. Circle punches are a favorite of mine, especially the 1½" and 2" ones. You could never perfectly cut a circle no matter how hard you tried. If the pages are not too thick, you can punch 2 at a time.

Burning windows is another favorite technique. Cut a hole smaller than the hole you want. Using incense or a butane lighter, burn bits of edging until shape is revealed. This can be a hit or miss technique, so be prepared to alter your plans if you burn a bigger hole than expected.

If you cut 2 pages together, you can sandwich different things between them. Vellum makes the next page seem misty. Here is a list of some of my favorites.

- • Netting • Sheer fabric • Clear plastic • Tissue paper
- • Thin rice paper • Tape or cold laminate transfer
- • Punch holes around window and sew a net or weave fibers.

Cut Holes, Windows, Niches & Shadowboxes

The King

MATERIALS: Book • Assorted rubber stamps • Black Memories ink • Sheer fabric (Vellum paper or mesh) • Collage elements (handmade paper, king picture, glossy pictures, calender page) • Fluid acrylics • Lumiere paint • Craft knife • Cutting mat • Bone folder or credit card • Glue stick

TIPS: Using a pencil and ruler, sketch a window shape. Place cutting mat under 2 pages, cut window and save the cutout.

Trim Vellum paper, mesh or fabric 1" larger than window. Open 2 pages so you have a window on each page. Put scrap paper under windows, apply glue around edges. Place Vellum, mesh or fabric over window, spreading it so it is taut. Completely cover other page with glue. Close pages and carefully smooth with bone folder or credit card. Paint pages and glue collage elements in place. Stamp as desired.

HINT: When you cut a window, you need to have some kind of image or quote to place in the window. This is called the payoff. If your payoff is uninteresting, people will not want to turn the page and see what you have done.

1. Mark the window with a pencil and a metal edge ruler.

2. Place a cutting mat behind pages to be cut. Cut with a sharp craft knife and a ruler.

Optional - Glue mesh, fabric or translucent Vellum paper between the windows.

Optional - Punch 2 pages with a giant punch and glue the vellum in place.

Mona

MATERIALS: Child's book • Collage papers• Alphabet and number rubber stamps • Cat's Eye pigment ink pads • Screens to sponge paint through • Old stamps • Cigar band • Glossy image of Mona Lisa • Lumiere paint

TIPS: When planning a collage, take preexisting windows into consideration. The windows are balanced with the large Mona Lisa element and the text background that is around the windows themselves.The glossiness of the Mona Lisa element is contrasted with the matte finishes of the text papers. Using postage stamps and background rubber stamps, bridged the windows and the Mona Lisa together.

The Hidden Face

MATERIALS: Book with niche • Gold print and Silver decorative paper • Gray cardstock • White paper • Rubber stamps (face, eye, 'confessions') • Brown stamp pad • Gold and Copper fibers • Gold eyelet • 26 gauge Gold wire • 28 gauge Silver wire • Copper seed beads • 1/16" hole punch • Foam sticky dots • Eyelet setter and hammer • Butane lighter

TIPS: Tear edges of decorative papers and glue on first page. Make opening for eye and burn edges. Stamp eye on White paper and glue behind opening. Cut flap to reveal title. Punch holes along edge and thread wire and beads. Cut door flap over niche opening. Insert eyelet and set. Tie fibers through eyelet and wrap top with wire. Stamp 'confessions' and face on Gray cardstock. Cut out. Glue 'confessions' on flap. Mount face pieces inside niche with sticky dots.

Tip for Smooth Edges

If you like the idea and look of a niche with smooth edges, a great artist, Pamela Burns, has come up with an easy way to cover those ruffled edges using heavy modeling paste from USArt Quest.

Create a Smooth Niche

Materials you will need are:
• Book with niche • Heavy modeling paste
• Acrylic paint or Lumiere paint • Gel medium
• Palette knife • Sandpaper

• TIPS: Work gel into the inside edges of niche and let dry. Once dry, scoop up a bit of modeling paste with palette knife. Using the straight edge of knife, fill cracks and creases with the modeling paste. Let dry.

Sand lightly. Run a small amount of modeling paste over the edges again. Sand lightly once more and paint.

Prepare a Deep Niche

Pick a book title that captures your imagination… then use the title as the design theme.

1. Clamp the pages together. Paint the edges with gesso.

2. Cut the niche with a craft knife and metal edge ruler.

3. Remove cut pages using the end of the craft knife.

4. Apply the gesso to the inside of niche opening.

5. Place mat behind page and cut door flap.

6. Glue door flap page to the niche frame.

Cutting a Niche ... a Deep Hole

A niche is a thick block of pages with a hole cut in it. Usually there is something three dimensional placed in a niche. The item doesn't have to be glued in. It's nice to encourage people to touch things in altered books.

• **Decide on the size and shape** of the niche. You can cut more than one niche in a block. Be sure that you have plenty of room around the niche. It should not be too close to the book's edge.

• **Determine how thick** the niche will be. Consider thickness of item placed in niche and thickness of book. Use a very sharp, heavy duty craft knife. Place a self-healing mat (or piece of cardboard) under the last page of block. Be sure to hold back page for front of the niche and a couple pages behind niche.

• **Clamp the block** or section with clothespins or binder clips.

• **Run gel medium** or tacky glue across outside edges of pages, let dry. Use a template or straight edge ruler and a sharp craft knife to cut out the niche pages.

• **For a board book** (a children's book with thick pages), cut one page at a time using a ruler or template as a guide. Glue pages together with gel medium, clamp and let dry.

• **For a very finished look**, insert a small box into the hole. Be sure to cut a hole in page which is the front of niche slightly smaller than the niche to cover uneven edges.

• **Color or finish the last page** before gluing the front, middle and back together. You can place almost anything in a niche:
• Small mirror • Art doll • Tag book • Letter game tiles
• Mini book or accordion book • Polymer or Paper Clay figures
• Flash card or altered playing cards • Crayons
• Charms • Round Glass to magnify words, phrase or picture.

More Fabulous Ideas for Glorious Niches

by Cindy Pestka

Display an ancient looking handmade globe with found objects from around the world to make a simple, elegant statement.

1784 Treasure Box

MATERIALS: Book • Textured paper to cover book • Embossed paper to cover spine • Snakeskin paper • Collage elements (2 playing cards, map paper, rolled magazine page tied with Gold cord, text paper) • Three dimensional elements (foreign coins, charms, chess pieces, cherub, bird, feather, half styrofoam ball, number and letter tiles, map in small Gold frame, bead) • 2 Gold tassels • Gold cord • Black flat braid • 24" of 6" Black tulle • Brown and Gold acrylic paint • Paintbrush • Glue stick • White glue • Hot glue • E6000

TIPS: Cover front and back of book with textured paper and spine with embossed paper. Highlight with Gold paint. Cut niche in book. Cover inside back cover with snakeskin paper. Wire pages together except for top two pages. Paint edges of niche Brown and highlight with Gold. Cover half ball with map paper. Glue half ball, bird and chess pieces in place. Thread tulle through arm of cherub. Glue ends of tulle to side and bottom of niche. Glue top pages over niche sandwiching tulle. Hot glue braid around edges. Glue cherub and charms to corners. Glue feather on tulle.

Glue text paper to inside front cover. Cut 4 triangles of textured paper and glue on corners. Glue collage elements as shown.

Thread center of tassel through bead, tie knots on each side. Glue braid, bead, number tiles, frame and charm in place. Highlight braid with Gold paint. Glue letter tiles on spine.

Nature is often hidden,
sometimes overcome,
seldom extinguished.
--Francis Bacon

Nature is Often Hidden
by Roben-Marie Smith

MATERIALS: Book • Dictionary page scraps • Old text paper • Assorted rubber stamps • Brown dye ink • Green and Mustard pigment ink • Coffee stained tags • Computer generated text on coffee stained tag • Tulle • Old pocket watch • Leaf • Ribbon • 6 Gold eyelets • Butterfly print napkin • Glaze paints • Green acrylic paint • Eyelet tool and hammer • Craft knife and cutting mat • Glue stick • E6000

INSTRUCTIONS: Glue last 50 pages of book together. Glue 2 sets of 2 pages together that come before the block. Do not glue to block. Let dry. Cut out niche in block using craft knife and cutting mat. Turn one 2 page set over top of block and cut opening. Paint left and right pages with pigment inks. Rubber stamp images on tags and page with dye inks. Paint with glazes to seal inks. Tear and place scrap paper and dictionary pages as shown. Cut napkin pieces and glue on page. Glue tag with quote on page. Attach eyelets to page sets. Glue inside edge of cutout niche with acrylic paint. Open glued pages to back cover. Glue script page to back cover so it shows through niche. Glue cutout pages to back cover. Glue watch, ribbon and leaf to the bottom of niche with E6000. Place tulle over niche opening and tape in place. Cover the wrong side of collaged niche page with glue, press firmly and hold in place until secure.

'Create'
by Beth Cote

MATERIALS: Board book • Handmade papers • Cardstock • Mulberry papers • Tags • Images from art book • *Stampington & Company* madonna rubber stamp • Assorted rubber stamps • Brown and Black Memories ink • Cat's Eye pigment inks • Computer generated quotes • Collage elements (measuring tape, old text, postage stamps, music) • Three dimensional elements (Letter game tiles, charms, rusty key, English coin, clay face, lock, beads, broken wax seal) • Fibers • Mesh • Lumiere paint • Brown Neopaque paint • Gesso • Gel medium • Gold pen • Very fine sandpaper • Wire • Awl • Craft knife • Krylon spray sealer

TIPS: Prepare board book. Glue with gel medium throughout this project.

Cover - Cut a hole through 2 pages in board book with craft knife to create a mini niche. The mini niche is a platform that makes collage elements seem more important without using as much space as a regular niche. Glue second page to the page behind it. Add old text. Stamp madonna on tea stained tag. Tear and burn tag to fit around niche. Glue on cover. Glue more text, folding edges of papers over spine. Sponge Lumiere paint through screens. Drill one small hole and push wire through hole to create tab.

Pages 2 & 3 - Paint page that you see through window Copper and Gold. Sponge Gold Lumiere through screen. Glue letter game tiles inside small niche on third page. Squeeze a bit of glue around letter game tiles and surround with small beads and broken wax.

Pages 4 & 5 - Glue image and quote on pages. Build up Brown paint over gessoed book and image. Stain quote and image with Brown paint to blend into picture wiping off excess paint quickly. Sponge Black and a bit of Copper Lumiere over pages.

Niche - Cut niche through pages. Glue handmade paper for background in niche. Paint with Lumiere. Add papers and quote on pages and around niche. Color over gesso and paper with Cat Eyes. Stamp images with Black Memories ink and heat set. Use Gold pen to make marks and swirls. Seal with spray sealer. This page will take a while to dry. Glue a bit of foam on back of rusty key. Let dry. Glue dimensional objects in niche. Collage back of book with various materials, then stamp and sponge Lumiere over them. Glue stamped and tea stained tag at the edge of book to create a closure that fits over wire on front. Punch small hole through cover of spine only and thread beaded fibers through opening. Paint small lock Gold and hang from frame.

Collage of Treasures

Add a touch of Midas to your decor with an opulent book overflowing with treasures. Glue all items on the page and in the niche, then spray paint everything gold for a Midas touch..

1. Glue niche block on book.

2. Glue the embellishments in place.

Golden Treasure Chest Book

MATERIALS: Book • Treasures (puzzle pieces, buttons, tassels, unusual coins, dominoes, chess and checker pieces, Letter game tiles, mah jong tiles, wood cutouts, jewelry, ribbon roses, plastic toys, dice, miniature wreath, flower pot, alphabet or number magnets, artificial fruit, miniature musical instrument, cherub head, brass charms, basket) • Gold spray paint • White glue • Hot glue

TIPS: Cut one large, deep niche in book leaving at least ¾" border on all sides. Wire pages together. Glue back of last page to back cover using White glue. Hot glue embellishments in and around window, on inside cover and top of book. Arrange treasures so they are layered and appear to tumble out of a crowded treasure chest. Spray paint entire book Gold.

NOTE: Even funky, tacky tidbits look elegant when painted Gold. This technique can also be used with cigar boxes, papier-mâché containers or small hat boxes. If you are using a deep container, glue a smaller box inside larger one so that you do not have to use as many embellishments.

1. Draw around a little tin box with a Black pen.

2. Mark the spaces for drawers on the inside of book with a Red pen.

Be creative with altered books...inset *real clock parts* into a niche hole!

Clock in a Book
by Beth Cote

If you happen to have a book with a beautifully engraved cover you are in luck! Now your can turn that cover into a clock that will showcase it's beauty and become a great family favorite.

Dream Clock Book
MATERIALS: Book with niche • Walnut Hollow clock kit and clock face • *Stampers Anonymous* dream placket rubber stamp • Brass 'dream' tag • Domino • Button • Garter hook • Awl • Gel medium
TIPS: Make sure that the thickness of the book is about one and a half to 2 times as thick as the box that holds batteries. Cut a niche in book that is larger than box. Stamp outside of book and make a hole through the book board. Attach the clockworks, clock face and hands to the outside of the book following manufacturer's instructions. Attach three dimensional objects. Do not glue book cover to inside of book since you will have to open it to replace batteries.

3. Cut out the drawers with a sharp craft knife and cutting mat.

4. Glue cut pages and edges of drawer openings.

5. Glue top pages of the book to the drawer edges.

6. Glue a button pull on the front of the tin boxes.

Little Drawers

by Beth Cote

Hide those special objects and make your altered book a hit using Altoid tins that have become little drawers with knobs opening to reveal a hidden shrine.

Altoid Tin Drawers

MATERIALS: Book • Altoid tin • *Oxford Impressions* rubber stamped images on old paper, enlarged and copied on acetate • Rubber stamps (*Ma Vinci's* remember, numbers) • Gold pigment ink • Vintage sewing supplies (old pattern pieces, hooks and eyes, snaps, buttons) • Rusting agent • Fluid acrylic paint • Charms, feathers and other 3 dimensional items • Paintbrush • Burnt Umber glaze • Diamond glaze • Gel medium • Spray sealer • 1¼" square punch • Metal ruler • Pencil • Craft knife

TIPS: Open book and trace Altoid tin at location of drawer. Be sure edge of tin is on edge of page. With another color, use a ruler and trace tin again adding ⅛" of extra space to both sides. The back of tin should still be flush with the original line. You need this extra wiggle room so drawers can move

in and out easily. Cut through pages of book with craft knife. Keep track of how deep you are cutting by placing tin in hole. When top of tin is just slightly lower than book, stop cutting. Glue pages and edges of niche. Let dry. Rust collage items and glue in tin. Open book to front pages and cut another thin niche in the beginning of book leaving 3 pages free. Glue and rip first 2 pages to create drape and punch square hole. Cut niche in last page for a frame to cover edges of transparency. Glue transparency over niche and glue free page over edges of transparency. Paint with fluid acrylics. Let dry. Add Gold pigment ink randomly. Add Raw Umber glaze over ink carefully as it will move ink. Glue another transparency to inside cover of book with diamond glaze. Glue pattern pieces to pages with gel medium. Spray to seal. Glue sewing supplies on pages.

'All My Favorite Shoes' Book of Many Windows

by Cindy Pestka and Sue Cramer

A book filled with a dozen colorful shoes will make the perfect gift for a shoe and accessories collector!

Shoe Store Book

MATERIALS: Book • Gold decorative paper to cover book • Black suede paper to cover spine • Glossy Gold background paper • Assorted decorative papers • 60" of 6" Black tulle • 2 Gold tassels • 2 buttons • Acrylic jewels • Rose and butterfly stickers • Aqua seed beads • Blue and multi glitter glue • 2 chopsticks • Swirl and ³⁄₁₆" square punches • Black spray paint • Gel medium • Gesso • Paintbrush • Hot glue

TIPS: Open the book to center. Mark the openings and cut windows the same size and depth on both sides of the book. Glue cut pages together. Paint edges with gesso. Spray paint Black. Insert background paper and glue in place.

Cover outside of book with Gold decorative paper and Black suede paper. Glue back of last page to back cover and back of first page to front cover.

Cut a shoe for each window from assorted decorative papers. Embellish with glitter glue, stickers, punched shapes, beads and jewels. Glue in place pointing in opposite directions. Wrap tulle loosely around chopsticks and loosely knot at ends. Hot glue to tops of pages. Tie tassels on chopsticks and glue buttons in place. Knot ends of tulle and hot glue in place.

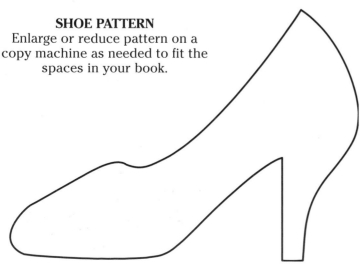

SHOE PATTERN
Enlarge or reduce pattern on a copy machine as needed to fit the spaces in your book.

Tips for Cutting Windows

• **Decide how many windows** your design will require and their location.

• **Decide if windows** will be shallow or go all the way through to back cover.

• **Lightly draw the window outlines** on the top page with a pencil, leaving at least a ³⁄₄" border on all sides.

• **Place a cutting mat** (or cardboard) between the last page that you want to cut and the remaining pages or the back cover so you don't cut too deep.

• **Cut the window to the desired depth** using a ruler and a craft knife.

• **Tips:** You can cut 10 to 20 pages at a time. Use a binder clip to hold cut pages to front cover so they are out of the way while you cut deeper pages. Remember only the cuts on the top page are completely visible, so you do not have to be too fussy about other pages, especially at the corners.

1. Mark off the opening using a pattern.

2. Apply glue around openings on pages.

3. Press borders on the 2 pages together.

4. Apply gel medium to edges of windows.

5. Spray paint Black.

6. Glue the Gold paper behind openings.

Flowing Water Mosaic

Flow a band of gleaming glass across your pages, then listen for the bubble of a clear, running stream.

by Cindy Pestka

1. Mark the design for water across pages.

2. Cut out the design.

3. Wire the pages together.

4. Glue the center pages down to cover the wires.

Flowing Water Book

MATERIALS: Book • Mesh to cover book • Egyptian images • Colored glass • Flat marbles • Charm • Mica tile • Skeleton leaf • 27" of Gold rattail • Silver spray webbing • Gold spray paint • White glue • E6000

TIPS: Open the book to center. Lightly sketch a design reminiscent of a flowing stream of water. Cut out between the lines about 1/4" deep. Spray paint the entire book Gold. When dry, apply Silver spray webbing to inside. Cover front and back of book with mesh. Wire pages together except for top 2 pages. Because cut portion extends to edge of pages, use 3 or 4 wires per page instead of just 2. Glue back of last page to back cover and first page to front cover with White glue. Glue top page to wired pages and press down firmly. Arrange glass and flat marbles in stream and glue with E6000. Apply collage elements with White glue. Glue charm in place. Glue 3 pieces of glass to support mica tile. Glue leaf on top of tile and tile on supports with E6000.

Create a Memorable Travel Journal

Moveable Art - Travel Journal

by Cindy Pestka

Recently I took a plain hardback book with me on vacation with the intention of recording highlights of my vacation using embellishments collected along the way. I brought along only a small box of basic supplies, White glue, glue brush, E6000, alphabet stamps, Black ink pad, scissors, plain paper tags, twine, needle and thread.

I began collecting images from maps, brochures, airline magazines and napkins that came with our meals. I picked up feathers, leaves, seashells, bits of sea glass and pottery.

Using fabric with a tropical motif I purchased in a small general store, I covered the book using the same technique described for covering a book with paper.

To the front, I attached twine threaded with seashells and coral collected on the beach and a tag with trip information. I also glued a fragment of coconut husk, a pottery shard and seashells on the cover. I glued lightweight embellishments, paper, feather and a silk flower and sewed on pressed leaves.

I even used small red berries to stain the background of some pages. Unused pages were folded in a simple alternating pattern to make the book more interesting. Folding completed pages also makes elements easier to find.

I added trip photos, notes and had people sign their names. I love reliving my trip when I look through this book.

I love re-living my trip when I look through this book.

Cindy

Treasure Box 'Book'

by Cindy Pestka

Create 'secret hiding places' for jewelry, money, love letters and valuables in these clever disguised 'book boxes'.

1. Cut all the pages from the book.

2. Cut the lid off the box.

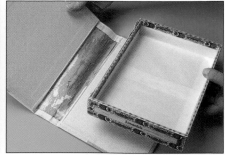
3. Glue box in the book.

Optional - Inside

You'll need a hand-covered book about ¾" thick and slightly larger than a VHS tape. Cut out all the book pages. Place a VHS case inside the book cover and glue in place. Paint or decorate the cover and sides as desired. You can keep valuables inside the case: jewelry, money, etc. Just keep the book in your library with the treasures 'safe' from would be thieves.

Glue a video tape box inside a book

Treasure Box

MATERIALS: Cigar box • Book slightly larger than box • Black embossed paper • Leather grain paper • Images from art magazine • Twine • Beads • Black acrylic paint • Paintbrush • Sandpaper • Craft knife • Hot glue

TIPS: Using craft knife, cut along front and back inside creases to remove pages. Using a craft knife, carefully cut the lid off box. Glue loose paper edges and lightly sand wood if necessary. Glue Black embossed paper on inside covers of book. Collage images on front cover. Sand spine to make the book appear old. Wrap twine around cover, thread beads on ends and knot to secure. Paint box Black. Glue leather grain paper around outside edges of box. Hot glue box in book with edge of box pressed firmly against inside spine. Hot glue back of box to back cover.

Make notes about each picture you snap and store related items in small envelopes in the book.

Hand-Sewn Journal

MATERIALS: Book with interesting cover • Cardstock • Decorative paper • Eyelets • Ribbon or cording • Beads or charms • Stickers, stamps or collage elements • Awl or hole punch • Craft knife • Strong tape • Glue stick

TIPS: Using a craft knife, cut along front and back inside creases to remove pages. If necessary, repair any weak or torn spines by running strong tape along length of weak area and glue ribbon or fabric inside.

Cut a strip of decorative paper the same length as book and twice as wide as spine. Glue over inside of spine. Using awl or hole punch, make holes 1" from top and bottom of spine and insert eyelets. Cut 2 pieces of cardstock or decorative paper slightly smaller than dimensions of cover and glue inside front and back covers, slightly overlapping paper covering spine.

To make 'signatures', first measure dimensions of opened book. Cut sheets of lightweight cardstock $\frac{1}{2}$" less than length and 1" less than width of book. Use 4 to 6 pages per signature. Fold sheets in half and punch holes to correspond with eyelets in spine. With sheets folded, trim pages so edges are even. The number of signatures will vary depending on size of book. Cut ribbon or cording about 4 times length of book and thread it through signature holes so tails are in back. Thread tails through eyelets in spine. When all signatures have been threaded, tie tails together near top hole to create an embellishment on outside of book.

Cut the ribbon tails to fall just above the bottom of the book. Add the beads or charms. Decorate the inside covers and pages with stickers, stamps or collage elements as desired.

Handmade Journal Book

by Cindy Pestka

Remove all original pages, then add pages of handmade paper for a beautiful book.

1. Cut the pages out of the book. Reinforce spine by gluing ribbon or sheer fabric inside spine.

2. Attach eyelets to the spine.

3. Glue end paper on the front cover.

4. Thread cord through the holes in a 'signature' of papers.

5. Thread cords through eyelets and tie ends together. Add beads.

"This journal is a book I made to spur me past those uninspired times. It combines some of my favorite illustrations and great quotes. It is enough to pull me out of any artist block and helps me remember exactly what is important and the real reason I do art."

How to Cut a Slit for a Tag

by Beth Cote

Cut the end off an envelope. Place a cutting mat behind the page and cut a slit. Align the cut end of the envelope with the slit and glue envelope on the back of the page.

1. Cut off the end of the envelope as shown here.

2. Place a cutting mat behind the page and cut a slit.

3. Align edges of the envelope with slit. Glue on back of page.

4. Glue the envelope page to the next page. Insert the tag.

TAG PATTERN

Fly away in dreams to uncharted lands and far-away seas.

Fly Away

MATERIALS: Book • Small envelope • Tag that fits envelope • Collage elements (map, postage stamp, pictures, receipt) • *A Stamp in the Hand* Chinese text rubber stamp • Cat's Eye pigment ink pads • Violet Earth Golden Glaze • Black Stabilo tone pencil

TIPS: Cut envelope so a bit of tag extends from opening. Cut flap off envelope. Trace opening of envelope with a pencil where slit will be located on page. Place cutting mat behind page and cut slit. Glue envelope on back of page aligning slit with opening of envelope. Glue pages together so envelope is sandwiched between pages. Turn back to front of page and slip tag into slit. Glue collage elements on page, paint and color with ink. Stamp text as desired.

Cutting an Opening with Doors

Cut an Opening

by Cindy Pestka

It is easy to use a stamp and make a shrine in your altered book. Depending on how you cut a stamped image you can make a slit, window, door, mailbox door, garage door or shutters from one stamp.

1. Stamp a frame and cut out the opening.

2. Cut a door in a stamped frame as shown.

3. Make a flap to fold up in a stamped frame.

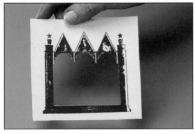

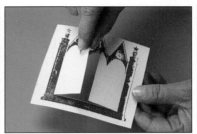

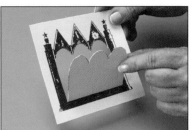

4. Cut around the stamped image to make a frame.

5. Cut a door in the stamped image as shown.

6. Cut a flap to fold down in the stamped image.

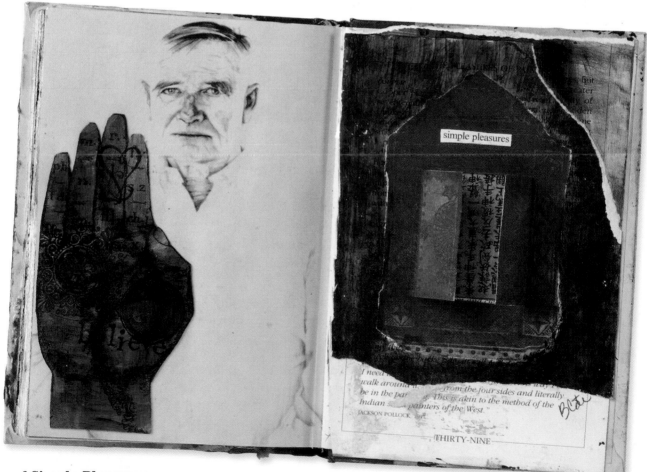

Shrine of Simple Pleasures

by Beth Cote

MATERIALS: White and Black cardstock • Chinese text paper • Extra book page • Acetate sheet • Rubber stamps (*Uptown Design* shrine of the divine, hand, heart, button, flower) • Face rubber stamp or face drawing • Cat's Eye pigment ink pads • Memories ink pad • Craft knife • Small cutting mat • Glue stick
TIPS: Stamp shrine on cardstock with Memories ink. Apply directly to shrine. Cut out shrine. Cut shutters with craft knife. The cut will look like a capital I. Trim Chinese text and acetate to fit window. Color backs of shutters. Layer and glue extra book page, background cardstock, Chinese text, acetate and shrine. Color page and background with ink. Glue on book. Stamp hand, flower and button with Memories ink and cut out hand. Glue on page.

How to 'Age' Book Pages

by Cindy Pestka

Add the romance of yesteryear to your altered books by aging them with our easy and quick techniques. The results are fantastic!

1. Glue the dictionary page in the book.

2. Glue triangles on the corners and curl up.

3. Dab ink on page with a stippling brush, add more ink near edges.

4. Sand the page lightly.

5. Spray the page with coffee or tea to age.

6. Sponge Brown glaze on page.

7. Glue the marble on the top center of the page.

8. Cut niches in book. Tear, curl edges, brush with Brown glaze.

How to 'Age' Papers

Vintage Dictionary

MATERIALS: Old dictionary, encyclopedia or science textbook or 2 dictionary pages and a second similar size book • Textured paper • Word rubber stamps • Black stamp pad • Small glass bottle • Bead to fit neck of bottle • Mica tile or thin plastic sheet • 3 Gold brads • 2 flat back clear glass marbles • African beads • 2 dried leaves • Stickers • Cream tulle • Small stone • Small hole punch • Hammer • Sandpaper • White glue • E6000

TIPS: Find 2 pages in book that capture your imagination. They might contain text, drawings or photographs that inspire you. If you don't want to use the entire dictionary or textbook, carefully cut out the 2 pages. Open second book to center and glue 2 pages on top making it appear that the entire book is a dictionary or textbook. Decide where windows and other embellishments will fit on page. Cut various size and depth windows large enough to hold treasures. Leave at least a ¾" border. Wire all pages together except top.

Choose collage elements and embellishments that relate to page. In a window, place a mysteriously labeled small glass bottle filled with sand. Glue bead in place instead of a cork. Cut irregular piece of mica tile or plastic sheet. Punch holes in tile and corresponding parts of top page and use small metal paper fasteners to secure. Tap fasteners lightly to flatten. Place marbles over words to magnify them. Glue African beads in one window and stone in other window. Attach remaining elements. Stamp words. Glue tulle over portrait stickers to soften appearance. Age collage elements, book pages and the cover if desired. Glue back of last page to back cover and back of first page to front cover with White glue. Cut 4 small triangles of textured paper and glue on corners. Roll edges of pages to age them. Glue top page to wired pages and press down firmly.

Tips for Aging Paper

Age collage elements and book pages by using any or all of these techniques. Do not be afraid to really work paper or pages for an authentic vintage look. Experiment on scrap paper until you find the look you like best.

• **Gently wrinkle** papers, then smooth.

• **Lightly rub** fine sandpaper over papers.

• **Using a makeup sponge** or stippling brush, apply and blend several shades of Brown, Tan, Yellow and Gray dye base rubber stamp ink directly on paper.

• **Use more near the edges.**

• **Place strong coffee** in a spray bottle and apply a few drops to paper. Wait for paper to dry before handling.

• **Curl or slightly tear** edges of paper.

Vintage Diary

MATERIALS: Hardback book • Decorative paper to cover spine • Vintage collage elements (key, receipts, tag, charm) • Color photocopies of photographs • Photograph • 2 Gold brads • Small hole punch • Paper fasteners • Hammer • White glue • E6000

TIPS: Cut 2 windows, one large enough to hold a photograph and another above it large enough to hold a key. Vary size and depth of windows. Make sure you have at least a ¾" border. Wire all pages together except for top page. Cover the spine. Glue collage elements in place. Glue back of last page to back cover with White glue. Punch small holes in top and bottom right corners of top page and insert brads. Lightly tap with a hammer to flatten and age brads. Glue top page to wired pages and press down firmly.

Age outer edges of book and inside windows. Tear a bit of the top page and age paper underneath. You don't want any part to look new.

NOTE: E6000 takes 30 minutes to set and objects can move around until glue dries. To prevent this, add a bit of hot glue to a small part of object and apply E6000 to remainder. Hot glue will hold an item in place until the E6000 dries completely.

Fabulous Vintage Ideas

Create the look of a really antique book. Combine the 'Aged Papers' look with Paper Collage, cut-out niches and fold-out messages.

Tips for Vintage Ideas

Combine 'Aged Paper' techniques with rubber stamps, and paper collage for really great looks.

Grand Rue
by Nancy Curry

MATERIALS: Book • Matboard scrap • *Art Impression* rubber stamp • Art emboss copper sheet • Metallic Copper floss • Metal alphabet set • Nickel brads • Brown acrylic paint • Acrylic glaze (Penny Copper, Deep Woods Green, Bark Brown) • Perfect Paper adhesive • Matte sealer • 1/16" circle punch • Cutting mat • Craft knife • Gel medium • Small piece of wood

TIPS: Clip 2 pages together with bull dog clips (large paper clips that snap together firmly). On first page trace outline of picture on second page. Cut jagged window. Place wax paper behind first page and paint Brown, let dry. Add Copper, Green and Brown glaze textural marks. Let dry. Add color highlights to picture with a small paintbrush and acrylic glaze. Let dry. Apply tape around back of window. Separate floss into one ply and cut 3" pieces. Attach to top vertically and then repeat horizontally. When complete, glue first and second pages together. Cut 1" x 2" piece of Copper sheet. Distress slightly by squeezing between hands. Place on wood and tap phrase into sheet using metal alphabet stamps. Punch holes in ends. Add paper fasteners and attach piece to slightly larger scrap of Black matboard. Glue on page. Add a vintage scrap image for interest. Seal page with matte sealer to prevent sticking.

Arm in Arm

MATERIALS: Book • Cat's Eye pigment ink pads • Black and White clip art or engraving from old book • Gold Golden Glaze • Black Stabilo tone pencil • 6 line size correction tape • Sponge • Gel medium

TIPS: Cut niche. Glue clip art inside opening and glue to back of book. Mask off any interesting text. Apply inks to paper in a random circular motion overlapping a bit. Apply glaze with a sponge and add Black Stabilo lightly to paper for interest. Let dry and unmask text.

Paper Collage

Create a book for the mentor in your life who has encouraged and inspired your ambitions.

Unfold childhood memories of long ago days

ABC Fold-Out Book
by Claudette Hunter

MATERIALS: Book • Alphabet paper • Brown/Black washi paper • 1¼" x 12" piece of White paper • Rubber stamps (A, B, C, *Catslife Press* 'altered book') • Black and Brown pigment ink • Black embossing powder • Photocopy of vintage photo • 2 large and 2 small washers • 2 Gold bells • Plastic paper clip • Press-on number • Fibers • Stipple brush • ¼" hole punch • Heat gun • Glue stick • White glue

TIPS: Stipple pages with Brown and Black ink. Stamp and emboss ABC. Tear washi paper and glue on pages. Glue 3 squares of alphabet paper on top of book. Glue 10 squares on one side of paper strip, fold accordion style and paper clip to page. Glue one square on front of accordion. Glue photo and large washers in place and apply number. Stamp 'altered book' on shrink plastic, punch hole and shrink. Tie plastic piece, bells and small washers on fibers. Glue the fibers along the crease.

Strong Women, Then and Now
by Claudette Hunter

MATERIALS: Book • Lacy washi paper • Vintage and modern woman images • Letter rubber stamps • Black and assorted color ink pads • Slide holder • Postage stamps • Sponge • Glue
INSTRUCTIONS: Sponge assorted color inks on pages. Glue images in place. Add lacy washi paper. Brush Black ink on a slide holder and glue over one photo. Add postage stamps. Stamp the title.

Fluid Acrylics and Glaze Mediums

by Beth Cote

Fluid acrylics and glazes work well with pigment ink to create fabulous looks.

1. Press a blob of paint between 2 pages.

2. Sponge glaze on a page.

3. Paint over screen lightly with acrylic paint.

4. Dab the ink on page with plastic wrap.

5. Dab Brown ink on the page with a sponge.

I use fluid acrylics and glazes in my work with pigment ink. Matte medium can be used as a glue for collage and mixed with acrylics to achieve transparent glazes. This is why I glue with matte medium when I collage. I paint with it and stamp with Memories ink without a problem.

Remember, matte medium has a tack and needs to be sealed with Krylon spray sealer, Golden varnish or, for a different look, buffed with spray furniture wax.

Beth

A mixture of inks and varnish creates an airy background. Pages are allowed to buckle creating an uneven background which lets ink seep into the pages. Varnish gives a soft sheen.

Lena

by Beth Cote

MATERIALS: Book • Ripped pieces of pages • Textured paper • Envelope • Asian and number rubber stamps • Fresco ink pads • Antiquing varnish • Gesso • Russet Lumiere paint • Pictures • Address label • Magic Mesh • Sponge
TIPS: Cut slit near top of right page. Align edge of envelope with slit and glue on back of page. Glue 2 pages together. Apply thick coat of gesso to make pages buckle. Let dry. Apply Fresco ink to page directly from pad. Apply in a rectangular motion mimicking shape of book. Do not cover page, let gesso show through. The ink should sit on the hills of buckles and work a bit into valleys. Apply second color of Fresco ink in a similar manner but only to accent first color. With sponge, apply varnish over entire page. Let dry. Glue collage elements in place. Apply Lumiere sponged through screens.

Aesthetic Components

Once you have the structure of a page or a series of pages planned or finished, it is time to turn your attention to the aesthetics. You can do just about anything to a page to get some color.

The one rule of thumb to remember is how pages wrinkle. The more moisture in a product, the more a page will wrinkle. Watercolors have a lot of moisture. Lumieres do not. To use watercolors on a page, collage the watercolor rather then use it directly in the book. Here are some preferred inks and paints.

• Lumieres & Neopaques • Golden fluid acrylics
• Any craft acrylic • Pigment inks • Dye-based inks
• Water-soluble oil pastels • Colored pencils • Crayons • Markers and gel pens.

Gesso pages before painting with acrylic to seal page and help prevent wrinkling. The page might wrinkle a bit at first, but as it dries it will flatten. Placing wax paper between pages and pressing with several heavy books can help.

Fluid Mediums

Simple elements make a dramatic statement. Here one collage image and Golden Glaze say it all!

Liberty

MATERIALS: Book • Golden Glaze (Indigo, Patina Green, Copper, Rust) • Statue of Liberty picture • Glue stick • Comb • Sponge • Knife or piece of matboard • Foam plate • Spray sealer

TIPS: Squirt Rust and Patina Green on plate. Pick up both colors with sponge and dab across both pages moving your hand randomly to cover any hard edges sponge may leave. Work Indigo into pages as well. Let dry and glue picture in place. Use glaze to cover part of picture. Using bottle spout, make a small line of Copper and Indigo glaze. Use a small piece of matboard or a knife to smooth into a streak. Use a comb to make interesting marks. Let dry. Spray sealer over the pages.

Elegance is the defining hallmark of a romantic page.

Beloved
by Claudette Hunter

MATERIALS: Cardstock • Alphabet rubber stamps • Black and Brown ink pads • Computer generated letter • Mini glassine envelope • Napkin or tissue paper • Girl image • Mica tile • Design Master Pink and Gold spray paint • Gold mesh ribbon • Gold heart charm • Postage stamp • Decorative scissors

TIPS: Spray pages with paint. Glue girl on page, cover head with mica tile. Add ribbon to opposite page. Add leaves cut from napkin or tissue. Cut cardstock with decorative scissors. Layer and glue cardstock and envelope. Tear the edges of the letter and rub with Brown ink. Insert in envelope. Glue charm and stamp in place.

Creating an 'Art Media' Chart

When altering books, it is important to know how paint, inks and other art media will work on collage material, book pages and with other paint. Creating a chart can help you remember how different paints work and inspire you to try new combinations.

MATERIALS: Paints & Inks (acrylics in tubes, acrylics in bottles, fluid acrylics, glazes, Black, Clear and colored gesso, permanent ink, pigment ink, acrylic inks used for calligraphy, walnut ink) • Pencils & Crayons (water soluble colored pencils, oil pastels, crayons, Stabilo Tone Metallic colored pencils) • Papers (book pages, glossy magazine pages, cardstock) • Glue stick

TIPS: Glue paper on black cardstock. • Add pencil and crayon lines down the page. Label each line. • Create a grid by painting a line of each paint and ink across the page. (You can mask the page to make straight lines.) • This chart makes it easy to be able to see how different mediums react with each other and different papers. Keep this chart handy.

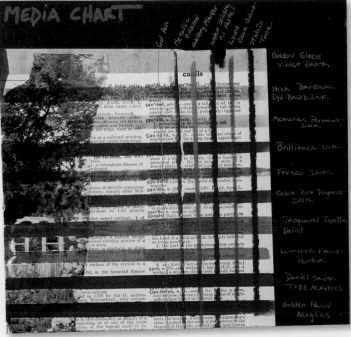

Lady in Clock Face

MATERIALS: Small book • Cardstock • Collage elements (text paper, old photo, quote printed on vellum, piece of old developed film, old foreign currency, postage stamp, ribbon) • Domino • Lady in a watch face • Clock face • Key • Face charm • Lumiere paint (Copper, Green, Gold) • Matches • Gold pen • Gel medium • Craft knife and cutting mat • Sponge

TIPS: Cut niche in book. Run marker over the edges of the book and paint book with Lumiere. Make a frame by folding text papers and gluing them around opening. Slip film into one corner under text. Glue photo on back inside cover and back cover to text block. Glue key and face charm inside niche with gel medium. Glue collage elements on inside front cover. Cut an irregular cardstock shape. Glue text paper and stamp on shape and ribbon under right edge. Sponge shape lightly with Gold and glue on front cover. Glue watch, domino and clock face in place. Fray ribbon edges.

Create beauty... combine photos, clock faces, dominoes and more!

Art Mini Book Cover

MATERIALS: Small book with niche • Old city scape photo • Brown ink • Button • Domino • Playing card • Face charm • 2 subway tokens • 18" of 1½" sheer Bronze ribbon • 10" of ⅛" Black/White woven ribbon • Small piece of 26 gauge wire • Small letter tiles • Black Lumiere paint • Paintbrush • Gel medium • Diamond Glaze • Copper pen

TIPS: Paint cover Black. Trim playing card to fit book, run Copper pen over edges and glue on book with gel medium. Edge sides of playing card with thin woven ribbon. Thread wire through button shank and curl to create a flat bottom. Glue wire and button on book. Sponge letter tiles with Brown ink and glue on domino with glaze. Glue domino to book. Layer face charm on top of 2 subway tokens. Glue together then glue on book. Glue Bronze ribbon ends on inside of covers.

From playing cards to old subway tokens, layering everyday objects can make your 'art' stand out.

Wonderful Mini Booklets

Tiny books... children's little books or small gift books often make wonderful projects that are quick to decorate.

1. Choose a small gift size book with a sturdy cover and lots of pages.

2. Cut a niche in the pages if desired. Paint, stamp and embellish book.

Mini Books
by Beth Cote

This is art: to fly toward a secret sky. To cause a hundred veils to fall each moment. Take a step without fear. A blank niche is enough to make anyone freeze. Start small using a mini book. Two to three things will fill up a niche and let you experiment with three dimensional items without a large empty space staring at you.

Beth

Hope is an eternal emotion springing even from a dark stamped forest background. On this cover, everyday items are transformed into beautiful art findings.

Hope Mini Book Cover
MATERIALS: Small book • Acetate sheet • Matboard • Collage elements (text paper, ticket stubs, dream charm, photo charm) • Rubber stamps (*Stampers Anonymous* tree branch, background) • Lumiere paints (Gold, Green, Black, Teal) • Button • Stick • Gold jewelry wire • Beads • Hand charm • Pasta alphabet • Gold pen • Rubber band • Paintbrush • Sponge • Gel medium • Craft knife and cutting mat

TIPS: Paint inside, side and outside book covers Teal and Gold. Lightly sponge Black on tree and background stamps and stamp images on acetate. Cut to fit front of book and back inside cover.

Wash stamps immediately. Glue tree on front of book and background inside back cover with gel medium. Cut niche in book. Glue alphabet pasta on small piece of matboard with gel medium and brush Gold paint over top. Run Gold pen over edges. Attach button, hand charm and matboard to cover.

Wrap wire around stick and thread with beads as you wrap. Attach stick to spine of book by threading a rubber band through spot where cover separates from spine of book. Stretch ends of rubber band out of book and wrap ends around top and bottom of stick. Tension will hold stick in place and the rubber band will be hidden. Glue collage text on inside cover. Trim a piece of stamped acetate and glue across corner of niche. Glue remaining collage elements referring to photo.

Pages 3 & 4 - Trace hand on a magazine photo for background. Cut out and glue to gessoed page. Stamp woman on cardstock and cut out. Print quotes on computer in different fonts and rip out. Burn the edges. Glue quotes, art and cardstock to the background. Screen Lumieres over both pages and sponge Gold Lumieres onto the quotes.

Tip

Do not try to cut any book into a shape with a hand-held electric saw. It gets too hot and the book may catch on fire.

Pages 7 & 8 - Punch a hole through 2 pages. NOTE: I step on my punch to do this and the punch may break after a while. You might want to cut the hole with a craft knife instead. Put screen between 2 pages and glue together. Trace hands on text pages and cut out. Glue on board book. Color pages with pigment inks. Stamp Da Vinci figure on handmade paper, cut out. Glue both images on book. Color quote with inks and glue over stamped figure. Add a bit of Mulberry paper to tips of fingers on right side then screen Bronze and Rust Lumiere paints on pages.

Pages 5 & 6 - Glue ripped text to right page. Stamp skeleton stamp on cardstock and rip into pieces. Cut apart Da Vinci painting and glue window to top of left page and lady to right page. Glue ripped pieces to both pages. Color empty places with Cat Eyes. Cover harsh edges with mulberry papers. Stamp Da Vinci text with Memories Black ink and heat set. Sponge Lumieres through the screens.

Pages 9 & 10 - Paint pages and stamp gears on background. Glue ripped text on left page. Glue lady on right page. Make hole in lower right edge. Tie fibers in hole. Tie beads and charms on ends of ribbon.

The Hand of Da Vinci

MATERIALS: Hand shaped board book • Matboard square • Spiral print tissue paper • Mulberry papers • Handmade papers • Cardstock • Da Vinci quotes • *Stampington & Company* Da Vinci rubber stamps • Cat's Eye pigment ink • Da Vinci Images from art book • Button • Fibers • Assorted beads • Hand charms • Small square of art glass • Magic mesh • Pasta letters • Button • Thread and needle • Book awl • Lumiere paint • Gel medium • Gesso • Very fine sandpaper • Butane lighter or candle lighter

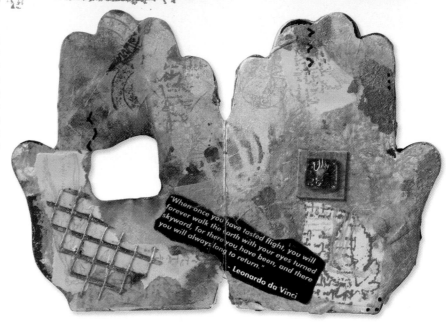

Hand Shaped Board Books

by Beth Cote

The shape gives your imagination a launch pad for creative ideas!

Board Book Basics

Board Books (children's books with thick pages) are slightly different than regular books when it comes to altering due to the glossy finish. Here are some steps to help with the problem.

- **Sand board book** up and down with fine grit sandpaper.
- **Sand pages from right to left** to create a cross hatch pattern that will help gesso & mediums adhere.
- **Use gel medium** to glue items.
- **Adhere lots of paper** and the paper will absorb the ink.
- **Use Lumiere paint** or Color Box inks on gessoed book board. Place a layer of medium over pigment inks and seal with spray sealer.

1. Sand pages up and down.

2. Sand from side to side.

Cover, Pages 1 & 2 - Cut a hole in board book with a craft knife. Collage old text from another book or use old pages from other niches you have cut. Use gel medium for glue. Stamp gears and Da Vinci handwriting on cardstock, tear out and glue on cover. Glue mulberry paper and printed tissue folding edges of papers over spine. Burn edges of window with lighter. Be careful while doing this, hold the book open and away from yourself over a sink filled with water. Sponge Lumiere paint through screens. Drill 2 small holes and sew button on cover. Cover matboard square with mulberry paper. Glue pasta letters in place. Glue charm on glass and glass in square. Center square in window and glue after collaging pages 1 and 2.

3. Clean the pages with a damp cloth.

4. Paint book with gesso.

Choose some text or words to highlight with paints, inks and masking. Accentuate the words to your own advantage.

1. Mask some words with correction tape.

2. Apply the ink to the page with a sponge.

3. Stamp an image on the page.

4. Remove tape.

5. Stamp again with a different stamp or ink color

Another component of altered books is the text (or words) on the page. By knowing and using transparent, semitranslucent and opaque mediums, you can manipulate the words to your advantage.

Showcase something special. Pockets and text highlighted with inks are easy ways to make additions to altered books.

Hand

MATERIALS: Book • Paper doll made with *Catherine Moore* character construction rubber stamps • Fibers • Peerless watercolors • Gold Pearl Ex • 4 Gold brads • Bead • Red Stabilo tone pencil • Needle or dental floss threader • ⅛" circle punch • Glue stick

TIPS: Glue 2 sets of 2 pages together for strength. Rip one set of pages from top of spine toward edge of book at halfway point. Holding both pages together, punch along outside edges where pages meet. Blanket stitch together with fiber. Start stitching at the spine. Tie off fibers and thread on a bead. Paint page as desired with watercolors. Do not attempt to use regular watercolors on a book page, they will buckle the page. Insert doll and hand in pocket.

Examples of Masked 'Text'

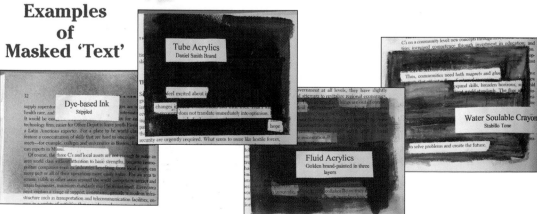

Masking the Text

Text is masked then highlighted for a poignant look. Buttons add texture and importance to the text.

We Do Not Remember *by Roben-Marie Smith*

MATERIALS: Book • Decorative handmade paper • Paper scraps • Rubber stamps ('We Do Not Remember', 'Lost Love') • Bronze pigment ink pad • Black dye ink • Old photos • Buttons • Color copy of cloth tape measure • Rust silk ribbon • Old key • ¼" hole punch • Spray sealer • E6000 • Glue stick

INSTRUCTIONS: Fold center page in half to create a triangle, glue. Coat left page and triangle with Bronze pigment ink, rubbing pad directly on paper. Seal pages. Glue photo, paper scrap, buttons and tape measure on left page. Stamp 'We Do Not Remember' with Black dye ink on folded page. Cover right page with decorative paper. Punch hole at top of page and tie ribbon through hole. Glue ribbon down side of page. Tie key on end of ribbon and glue key on page. Add other photo to the back of triangle. Stamp 'Lost Love' with alphabet stamps and Black dye ink on decorative paper.

Tips for Masking 'Text'

Masking is a way to use the text and pictures in a book. I use correction tape and cover-up tape in one, 2 and 6-line widths.

Phrases tend to jump out at me from the text and I'll use them as a basis for my collage. Found poetry is fun and easy to do. Pick out and mask words. Paint page and when finished lift off the tape.

I also like to incorporate drawings or art that might already be in a book. Masking the page helps me use the art to my advantage.

Crumpled tissue paper in multicolors makes an excellent page background to highlight cut out text.

Happiness
by Claudette Hunter

MATERIALS: Book • Multicolor tissue paper • White paper with computer generated text • Gold textured sequins • Gold Rub 'n Buff • Sponge • White glue

TIPS: Tear tissue paper in pieces and strips, crinkle and glue on pages. Highlight with Rub 'n Buff. Glue sequins in place. Trim text and glue on page.

Folded Pages

This fun and easy book sculpture is a great way to display photos, tickets, tags, Christmas cards and a personal collection of memorabilia. Keep it on a coffee table to display your favorite photos.

Photo Holder for Coffee Table

by Beth Cote

MATERIALS: Thin book • Handmade papers • Sheet music • Postage stamp • Calling card • 5 small candle cups for feet • Gold Lumiere paint • Paintbrush • Hot glue

TIPS: Paint cover and feet Gold. Fold all pages into triangles by folding top of page down into spine and bottom of page up into spine. Glue collage element on inside of both book covers. Hot glue feet on corners and spine of book. Fan pages out. If book is new, the spine might have to be broken a bit. Also, older books might tear a bit at edges which is fine. Arrange photos between pages.

Wishcraft

by Lenna Andrews Foster

MATERIALS: Thin book • White cotton fabric • Tickets • Fortune • Chinese coin • Glitter • Clipolas • Border stickers • Fibers • Rubber stamps by *LennaLines* and *Stampsmith* • Dye inks (Blue, Yellow, Turquoise, Amber, Brown) • Gold and Metallic Russet Lumiere paint •

TIPS: Glue two pages together and cut into a tag shape. Stipple dye inks across the pages starting with the lightest color, then working into the Browns. Lightly spatter Turquoise inks across pages. Mask text, then smear Lumieres across bottom of right page. Let dry.

Take tape off and edge masked area with glitter. Stamp cotton cloth with Fabrico fabric inks. Edge the pages with the border stickers and glue fabric, ticket, clipolas and fortune to pages. Stamp with Lenna Lines quote stamps across pages. Glue fibers down the middle of the pages.

Envelope Keepsake Book
by Cindy Pestka

MATERIALS: Book with interesting cover • Light Blue cardstock • Assorted envelopes • Stickers • Fibers • Beads • Strong tape • Craft knife • Awl • Double-stick tape

TIPS: Using a craft knife, cut along front and back inside creases to remove pages. If necessary, repair any weak or torn spines by running strong tape along length of weak area.

Cut 2 pieces of cardstock slightly smaller than dimensions of the cover and glue on inside front and back covers.

Then make an accordion spine to hold the envelopes. Determine the number of envelopes (an odd number works best). Plan for a ¾" accordion pleat for every envelope, plus two additional ¾" pleats at each end. Cut cardstock to this length, and make the height slightly less than the book. Glue the first and last pleats to the cover and tape the closed side of envelopes to front and back of the remaining pleats.

Use awl to make a hole in upper right corner of front cover. Cut fibers about 2½ times length of book and thread through hole knotting on both sides. Cut tails to fall just above bottom of book. Add beads, knot to secure. Attach stickers to envelope flaps.

Envelope Keepsakes

Fill a book with envelopes, then keep precious photos, notes and letters inside.

1. Glue the accordion folds inside the book.

2. Glue 2 accordion folds together for strength.

3. Punch a hole in the cover for threading fibers.

Honeycomb Pockets
by Beth Cote

MATERIALS: Book • 4 to 6 Coin envelopes • Copy of a furlough paper • Computer generated words • Personal Stamp Exchange ink bottle rubber stamps • Cat's Eye pigment ink pads • Circle template • Fibers • Small rectangle hole punch • Glue Stick

TIPS: Pick pages with printed images. Color with ink pads. Cut hole left page. Glue furlough and words on page and color edges. Stamp image above hole.

For honeycomb, cut off ends of coin envelopes 1/2" shorter than width of book. Place an oval-shaped spot of glue in the center of an envelope and place next envelope on glue. Repeat for all envelopes. Let dry.

To cover honeycomb, find 4 empty pages in book. Glue sets of 2 pages together for strength. Let dry. Measure book lengthwise and mark location of honeycomb. Cut excess page away leaving only cover of honeycomb. Punch edges and add fibers. glue end envelopes inside covers. Let dry.

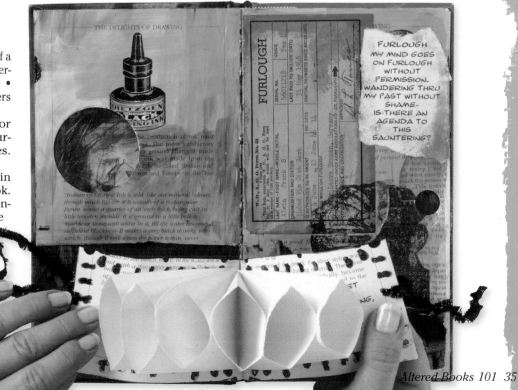

A stately woman stamped on a tag, music and gold accents make a page to fill the soul with song.

Song of the Soul

MATERIALS: Book • Collage elements (printed tissue paper, sheet music) • *Oxford Impressions* beloved plate rubber stamp • Fresco ink pads • Tag • 26 gauge Copper wire • Beads • Clear Golden Glaze • 1/8" circle punch
TIPS: Apply Fresco inks randomly on tag and stamp image with darker ink. Punch 4 holes in tag and page. Thread wire through the holes. Bead and curl ends of wire to secure. Glue collage elements on page behind the tag. Glaze page.

See instructions for ripping page edges on page 37.

See instructions for ripping page edges on page 37.

Trim Tip
Glue a reinforcement strip of paper on the top of a page. Sew sequins in place. (see below)

A gypsy's pocket is always filled with good fortunes. Just add words, wishes and whimsies.

Gypsy   by Karenann Young

MATERIALS: Book • Gypsy images from ARTitudeZine.com • Little girl images from ARTchix Studio.com • Rubber stamps on fortune telling cards from ARTchix Studio.com • Other images and text from Dover clip art & computer generated • Large sequins • Sewing thread & needle • Rust acrylic paint • Sponge
TIPS: Assemble the page referring to the photographs.

Lend a feeling of nostalgia with a doily painted with Lumiere.

A family photo adds the right central image to this romantic glimpse of yesteryear.

Walking Down the Aisle

MATERIALS: Book • Collage elements (handmade paper, text papers, label, pictures, printed vellum) • Assorted envelopes and tags in various sizes • Rubber stamps (French words, Eiffel Tower, floral background) • Brown Memories ink • Plastic doily • Metal tag with number • Enlarged copy of a photo • Yellow fibers • Gold Lumiere paint • White acrylic paint • Golden Glazes • Gel medium • Butane lighter • Paintbrush
TIPS: Paint doily Gold. Glue collage elements on pages. Glue words on vellum envelope and paint larger envelope White. Stamp tags with French words, Eiffel Tower and floral background.

Rip corner off large envelope. Glue envelopes on page (see page 39). Glue metal tag on envelope. Insert medium and large tags into envelopes.

Cut out photo, fold crease and glue in place. Glue envelopes on page. Trim doily and glue on page with gel medium. Sponge edge of page with Lumiere paints. Burn edges of one page. Tie fibers on one tag and place tags in envelopes.

Creative Edges for Pages

Ripping adds texture and interest to pages. Rip with the clean edge or ragged edge up. To rip with a clean edge, pull page toward you. Place a word, poem, a stamped image or a picture under the ripped page.

Anyone would love this book filled with nostalgic sewing notions.

Ripped Series of Pockets

MATERIALS: Book • Collage elements (woman picture, text papers, playing card, mulberry paper) • Pocket elements (photos, playing card, 2 tags, package of snaps) • Rubber stamps (butterfly, art, Eiffel Tower, postage) • Black and Brown Memories ink • Golden Glazes • Beads • Charm • 28 gauge Copper wire • Gold fluid acrylic • Red backed double-stick tape • Copper paint pen • Spray sealer

TIPS: Follow instructions for making ripped pockets. Collage woman, ripped playing card and other text papers to plain page and between ripped pockets. Apply glazes and fluid acrylics over collage elements.

Let dry. Stamp Black butterfly and art stamps with Black. Surface is bumpy and most stamps will not stamp clearly creating an uneven aged look. Rip mulberry paper into strips and glue around image to partially frame. Spray with sealer.

Stamp Eiffel Tower and postage stamp on tags with Brown ink. Edge with a Copper pen. Tie fibers, charm and small tag on a large tag.

Attach fibers to top of tag and tie to the folded pages. Attach beads to the ends of fibers with wire. Insert pocket elements in pockets.

Ripping Page Edges - Pockets

1. Rip the last page for the shallowest pocket. Continue to rip pages graduating as you go forward.

2. Tape or glue the top and bottom edges of the pages together to make pockets.

Folding Page Edges - Attach Tag

1. Fold and glue page in fourths.

2. Mark holes on tag and page.

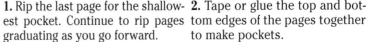

Paper Dolls
by Beth Cote

MATERIALS: Book • Mulberry paper (Purple, Orange, Green) • 2 pages of text • Blue paper shreds • Small drawing • White paper • Rubber stamps (butterfly, dragonfly, fish) • Black Memories ink • White gel pen

TIPS: Cut window in one page. Stamp fish on White paper, cut out. Glue text on page. Glue fish and drawing on page. Tear mulberry paper and glue on pages. Stamp dragonfly and butterfly on pages and glue additional mulberry paper and paper shreds in place. Cut a chain of paper dolls from text page Glue first and last dolls on page. Write message with a gel pen.

Come Play with Me
by Karenann Young

MATERIALS: Book • *ARTchix Studio* Little Girl Images and rubber stamps • Painted Gold dollies • Punched text stars • Background images from old book • *Dover* clip art • Yellow and Brown Paint • Glue

TIPS: Assemble the page referring to the photographs.

Lady of Leisure

MATERIALS: Book • Mulberry paper for hinge • Collage elements (printed paper, extra book page, postage stamp, pictures, money, old dress pattern pieces) • *Stampers Anonymous* frame rubber stamp • Art doll • Fluid acrylic paints • Gold Lumiere paint • Gel medium

TIPS: To make a fold-out page (see page 39), cut a piece of mulberry paper 2" wide and 1" shorter than extra page. Fold mulberry paper in half lengthwise for hinge. Attach half of hinge to back of extra page. Attach other half of hinge to back of page in book. Glue back of page to next page in book so mulberry hinge is sandwiched between pages. You can add more than one page to a spread this way. They can overlap and open from the top, bottom and side. Glue background collage elements in place. Color with acrylics. Glue piece of page, postage stamp, stamped pattern piece and art doll in place. Highlight with Gold paint.

HINT: It's fun to stamp on dress pattern pieces. They become semitransparent when glued and can pick up the finest details from a stamp. If your collage is bumpy, it's a good way to add a clear stamped image.

Not only can tags and envelopes be used as design elements, but in Lady of Leisure, a little art doll adds an extra element that is fun and sophisticated.

Add other art elements that you get from friends and swaps. This little art doll was made by Jackie Deeks.

Tags are one of the most useful elements in altered books. In addition to using them in pockets, gluing them on the page and tying them to fibers so they flutter when they hang out of the book, you can punch holes in book pages and dangle them. Think about using different shapes like metal ringed tags, several tags and eyelets to strengthen holes.

Easy to Believe in Ideals

MATERIALS: Book • Collage elements (postage stamps, text paper, printed paper) • Purple mulberry paper • Layaway tag • *Stampington & Company* assorted rubber stamps • Crimson fluid acrylic paint • Chinese character punch • 1/8" hole punch • Scissors • Glue stick

TIPS: Glue 2 pages together. Cut pages 1/3 down from top. Cut away from spine carefully leaving a bit of page hanging. Do not get too close to spine or you will cut into binding. Glue collage elements in place. Punch hole in top 1/3 of page and tie on stamped tag. Stamp 'believe' on printed paper. Paint page behind dangle with fluid acrylics. Punch with Chinese punch and glue mulberry paper behind page.

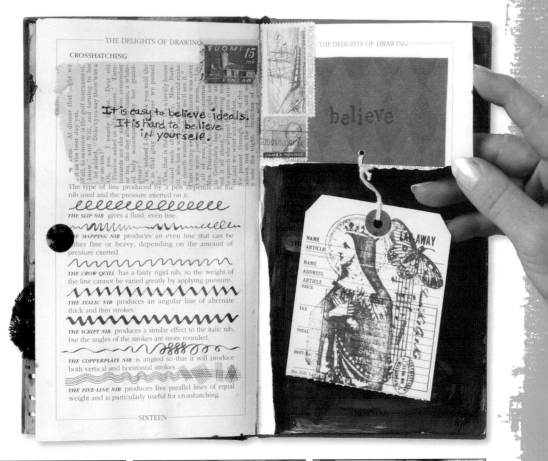

Tags & Envelopes

by Beth Cote

Tags make fabulous design elements! Add notes, happy thoughts and other art elements from friends and swaps.

1. Glue 2 pages together to strengthen the paper.

2. Cut off the bottom two-thirds of the glued page. Discard it.

3. Glue a tag to hang from the top one third of remaining page.

Folding Pages & Parts of Pages

The easiest way to alter a book is by folding pages. You are probably an expert having dog-eared a novel once or twice in your life.

The important thing to remember about altering is, if you have a flap, you need to have a payoff… something interesting under the flap that rewards the reader when they look. It can be as simple as a poem or picture. It can be a hole that gives you a peek into the next page or a pop-up.

Don't think that folding stops at making a flap, see how many different folds you can use. Dangle something from points of triangles or fold a page into thirds and sew a tag on the point.

Making a Fold-Out Page

1. Glue a folded strip of paper (or mulberry paper)to edge of page.

2. Glue straight edge of torn page to folded paper for hinge.

Helpful Hints:

Tip - Glue an envelope on the page.Insert a tag, photo or note.

Tip - Apply glue to page. Attach tags, envelopes or images.

More Great Ideas for Altered Books & Pages!

by Claudette Hunter

An old tape measure accents childhood and adolescent photos.

Growing Up
MATERIALS: Book • Map scraps • Old photographs • *A Stamp in the Hand* background rubber stamp • Brown and Black ink pads • Pink vinyl sheet • Mini tape measure • Gold eyelet • 3 buttons • Raw Umber acrylic paint • Paintbrush • Eyelet tool and hammer • Xyron machine • Glue stick • White glue

TIPS: Stamp background on pages with Brown ink. Laminate one photo, and map scraps. Glue laminated materials on right page. Insert eyelet at top of plastic. Antique measuring tape with Burnt Umber. On left page, glue measuring tape, photo and buttons. Stamp title with Black ink.

Be… live up to your potential.

Be
MATERIALS: Book • Lavender lacy handmade paper • Vellum • Letter rubber stamps • Black pigment ink pad • Black embossing powder • Pictures of dancer and woman's face • Mini mirror • Gold mesh • Yarn (Red, Green, Purple) • Assorted beads • ¼" hole punch • Purple Design Master spray paint • Heat gun • Large eye needle • Double-sided tape • Glue stick • White glue

TIPS: Spray paint pages. Stamp and emboss BE on vellum and cut to fit page. Cut out dancer pictures. Tear edges and glue handmade paper on left page. Glue dancer pictures near bottom of page and tape vellum in place. Cut out woman picture. Glue picture, mirror and mesh on right page. Holding 3 right pages together, trim slightly. Punch holes down side. Blanket stitch pages together leaving yarn tails at ends. Thread beads on tails and tie knots to secure.

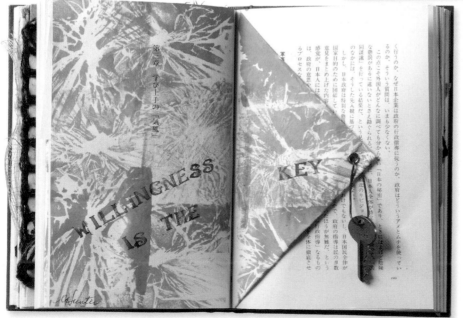

Folding is the key to this simple yet elegant design.

The Key
MATERIALS: Book • Rubber stamps (alphabet, moldable foam impressed with raffia bow) • Mustard and Black ink pads • Gold eyelet • 24 gauge Red wire • Key • Eyelet tool and hammer • White glue

TIPS: Stamp pages with molded foam and Mustard ink. Fold one page into triangle and set eyelet in point. Attach wire and key. Stamp Black title. Glue point of triangle on page.

More Great Ideas for Altered Books & Pages!

Luxurious fibers and colored tissue paper make a dramatic page. Tuck friendship quotes in the pocket.

Friends

MATERIALS: Book • Multicolor tissue paper • Dark Red cardstock • Burgundy ink pad • Printed text • Photocopy • Fine Gold cord • Purple fibers • Yarn (Red, Green, Purple) • Assorted beads • ¼" hole punch • Xyron machine • Needle and large eye needle • Double-sided tape • Glue stick • White glue

TIPS: Fold 2 pages back on themselves to make pocket. Glue edges. Rub with stamping ink. Glue tissue paper across page. Xyron photo and attach to page. Attach fibers with tape. Cut out printed text, glue on cardstock and laminate. Thread needle with cord and attach to cardstock to make tags. Holding 3 left pages together, trim slightly. Punch holes down side. Blanket stitch pages together leaving yarn tails at ends. Thread beads on tails and tie knots to secure. Insert tags in pockets.

Mystery abounds in this black and white design.

Who Am I?

MATERIALS: Book • Tissue paper • Large letter and face rubber stamps • Brown and Black ink pads • Silhouette of a woman's face • Black and White photo of a woman's eye • Small mirror • 2 flat back Clear marbles • Glue stick • White glue

TIPS: Stamp 'WHO AM I' on tissue paper and cut out. On left page, stamp a Black and Brown face. Glue marbles over faces and words on page. Cut out silhouette and eye. Glue eye on silhouette. Glue silhouette and mirror on right page.

Simple elements and paint effects make this single page truly dramatic.

Z Face

MATERIALS: Book • Library book pocket • Cream paper • Rubber stamps (*The Studio* Z face, *Stampers Anonymous* crackle) • Ink pads (Black, Brown, Terra Cotta) • Paper game piece • Brass watch parts • Black fiber • Charm with dangle • ¼" hole punch • Glue stick • E6000

TIPS: Stamp background on page and book pocket using Terra Cotta and Brown inks. Stamp crackles using Black ink. Stamp Z face on Cream paper, tear edges and rub with Brown ink. Glue book pocket, Z face and watch parts on page. Cut game piece to fit book pocket, punch hole and attach fibers and charm. Insert in book pocket.

Covering the Outside of a Book

by Cindy Pestka

Create a romantic lead in by embellishing the cover of your altered book. Add paint and accessories... and it is always fun to include the original title.

Cut 2 rectangles of paper about 2" longer and wider than book cover. Use art paper, wrapping paper or fabric. With White glue, attach one sheet to outside of front cover. Place one long edge of paper near crease where book bends and let the rest extend evenly beyond 3 edges of cover. Trim corners at an angle. Turn over edges of paper to inside and press firmly. Repeat for back.

• **Cut or tear a strip** of contrasting paper about 3 times width of book spine and about 2" longer than book. Glue strip centered over spine with long edges extending over paper applied to front and back covers. Cut excess off at top and bottom or fold edges to inside and press down firmly. If you fold edges, snip paper straight down to where book creases. This will make it easier to push edges of paper inside spine.

• **For inside front cover,** cut a rectangle from same or complementary paper about ¼" smaller than dimensions of cover. Glue to inside front cover and press down firmly. This piece will cover the edges of outer cover paper. For inside back cover, cut a piece of paper 1" smaller than cover and glue. Press down firmly. This paper will be background for windows. If you made windows that do not extend to back cover, glue background paper behind window on page where you stopped cutting.

• **Instead of covering entire outside** of book, cover just the spine. You can even add a title using fancy writing, computer generated text, rubber stamps or transfer letters. Paper covering spine of book can have torn edges or have holes torn to reveal part of actual title of book. Beads can be sewn to paper before gluing. You can also use this technique to cover unaltered books. Imagine personalizing a favorite book by covering it with beautiful papers or decorating a scrapbook or journal.

• **If desired, spray paint** book. You can paint the entire book or just the inside, then cover the outside with paper or vice versa. Or wait until all embellishments have been added, then spray paint book.

1. Align the paper edge with the edge of the spine.

2. Miter the corners and turn paper to inside of cover.

3. Mark the spine paper.

4. Method 1 - Cut off excess and glue (perfect paper adhesive is good) center of paper on spine.

5. Method 2 - Insert flap in space between spine and pages.

6. Glue paper on inside front cover and background paper on inside back cover.

Plastic wrap becomes an art form when filled with a romantic saying plus bits of crayon, beads and string.

Aspire to Be
by Beth Cote

MATERIALS: Book • Blue tissue paper • Printed paper • White paper • *Uptown Design* 'aspire to BE' rubber stamp • Brown Memories ink • Plastic wrap • Bits of old crayons • Buttons • Metal seed beads • String • Gesso • Heat gun • White glue • Glue stick

TIPS: Stamp words on White paper, cut out. Sandwich bits of crayons and string, seed beads and bits of printed paper between plastic wrap. Use heat gun to melt wrap and crayons, creating a web effect. Cut or tear a window in center of web. Glue words and web on top of tissue paper that has been crinkled and glued on book cover. A very light coating of gesso highlights the wrinkles of the tissue. Glue buttons in place.

Add sparkle to book covers with beads and everyday objects like bottle caps. If you can't find bottle caps at your local craft store, try a wine making store.

Hand

MATERIALS: Book • White tissue paper • Word cut from magazine or printed on computer • Beaded hand • Gold seed beads • Bottle cap • Water soluble oil pastels • Diamond Glaze • Gloss or matte medium • Gel medium • Gesso • Craft stick

TIPS: Crumple tissue paper. Apply gesso to book cover then cover gesso with tissue. Let tissue form ridges and valleys. Carefully apply gesso on top of tissue. Let dry. Rub pastels over ridges and valleys. Scrape off sections of pastel with craft stick. Seal with gloss or matte medium. Pour beads into bottle cap to cover bottom. Carefully drip Diamond Glaze over beads until beads are covered. Place cut out word on top of beads and let dry overnight. Glue beaded hand and bottle cap on book cover with gel medium.

Simple Abundance Artbook

MATERIALS: Book • Cardstock • Letter stamps • Watch face • Seed beads • Broken wax seal • 4 Gold eyelets • Eyelet setter and hammer • Lumiere Paints (Purple, Black, Copper, Gold, Light Blue) • Magic Mesh • Gel medium • Craft knife • Sandpaper • Sponge

TIPS: Cut square window in cover with craft knife. It should take about 3 repeated cuts to get through book board. Lightly sand book cover. Paint Purple avoiding text on cover that you want to keep. Sponge Black, Copper and Light Blue through Magic Mesh. Glue mesh in place with gel medium and sprinkle beads and wax on top of gel. Glue word over title.

For inside cover, cut a piece of cardstock to fit window. Collage with papers and add paint for a decorative finish. Glue watch face on top with gel medium then glue cardstock on book. Print dedication on cardstock, cut out and attach to page with eyelets.

Courage is the theme. Add apron strings to the wooden doll body.

The apron moves to reveal a quote by Goethe. 'Whatever you dream, begin it. Boldness has a genius, power and magic in it.'

Dreams

MATERIALS: Book • Wood doll shape • Tag • Small rubber stamps • Black Memories ink • Small letter tiles • Round mirror • Pony beads • Fibers • Button • 24 gauge Copper wire • Washer • Acrylic paint • Diamond Glaze • Gold gel pen • Craft drill and bit • Sandpaper • Gesso

TIPS: Sand and apply gesso to doll. Paint with acrylics, let dry. Draw designs with Gold pen, stamp with Memories ink and heat set. Apply Diamond Glaze over doll and set mirror and seed beads in glaze. Let dry. Stamp tag and apply a coat of Diamond Glaze. Drill small hole for tag in doll. Run Copper wire from back of doll through tag and one hole of button. Go back through other hole, hole in tag and hole in doll. Secure wire. Add beads and washer to fibers. Attach fibers to wire between tag and doll body. Glue doll to book cover. Ink letter tiles and glue in place.

Creativity

Take the realm of self-help books one step further.

What better way to brighten your life than to alter a book?

Beth

Today and Tomorrow

 al-ter (ôl′tẽr), *v.t.* and *v.i.* to change; make or become different; as, she *altered* the dress; his manners *altered* for the better.

 be-lieve (bḗ-lēv′), *v.t.* [believed, believing], **1,** to accept as true; as, I *believe* part of the evidence; **2,** to trust the word of; place confidence in.

 cre-ate (krḗ-āt′), *v.t.* [creat-ed, creat-ing], to cause to come into existence; make; originate; produce; also, to cause; occasion; as, to *create* a disturbance.

 des-ti-ny (dĕs′tĭ-nĭ), *n.* [*pl.* destinies], **1,** lot or fortune; fate; as, it was his *destiny* to die alone; **2,** the succession of events in life considered as something beyond the power or control of man; as, it is folly to whine against *destiny*.

 dream (drēm), *n.* **1,** thoughts, feelings, or pictures experienced or seen during sleep; **2,** something imagined; as, a *dream* of greatness:—*v.t.* [*p.t.* and *p.p.* dreamed (drēmd) or dreamt (drĕmt), *p.pr.* dreaming], **1,** to see, think, or feel during sleep; **2,** to imagine or hope for.

 **im-age** (ĭm′ĭj), *n.* **1,** a statue, bust, or similar representation of a person or thing; as, an *image* of the Virgin Mary; **2,** a close likeness; as, he is the *image* of his brother; **3,** a mental picture; an idea; **4,** a reflection in a mirror or something seen through a camera lens, magnifying glass, or the like:—*v.t.* [imaged, imag-ing], **1,** to form a likeness or picture of (something); portray.

IMAGE OF BUDDHA

 im-ag-ine (ĭ-măj′ĭn), *v.t.* and *v.i.* [imagined, imagin-ing], **1,** to form an idea or mental picture of (something); **2,** to suppose; fancy.

 love (lŭv), *n.* **1,** fond and tender attachment; as, mother *love*; also, passionate devotion; **2,** strong liking; as, *love* for music; **3,** a sweetheart:—*v.t.* [loved, lov-ing], **1,** to have a feeling of deep affection for; as, I *love* my sisters; **2,** to delight in.

 pas-sion (păsh′ŭn), *n.* **1,** any intense feeling or emotion, as joy, fear, love, etc.; **2,** an outburst of rage; **3,** love; intense desire; enthusiasm; as, a *passion* for music; **4,** the object of love, interest, etc.; as, poetry's my *passion*; **5,** passions, the emotions.

 vi-sion (vĭzh′ŭn), *n.* **1,** the sense of sight; also, the act or faculty of seeing; sight; as, the accident impaired his *vision*; **2,** that which is seen in a dream or trance; as, the *visions* of a prophet; also, a phantom; **3,** a mental image; a picture created by the fancy; as, a boy's *visions* of glory; **4,** imagination; foresight; as, a leader must be a man of *vision*.

 **vis-u-al-ize** (vĭzh′ū-ăl-īz), *v.t.* and *v.i.* [visualized, visualiz-ing], to form a mental picture (of); see in fancy.

Collage Clips
Copy these images on
a black and white copier.
Use them to decorate your pages.
(See page 2 for copy permission guidelines)

Transfer images and includes permission free materials and images used by permission of Dover Pictorial Archive Series • Dover Clip Art Library

Betty liked to go
to school
and she liked reading too,
'Bout fairy queens and
princes
and all the things they do.

Sometimes Betty'd make believe
she was a princess fair,
For Betty Jane had
big blue eyes

Curiosity Department

Q & A
by Beth Cote

What if you make a mistake?

There are no mistakes, remember! But, if you do something you don't like, here are some ways to fix it.
• **Keep adding.** Sometimes when a page isn't right, it needs just a little something extra like rice paper glued over something bold or a wash of matte medium and acrylic paint to mute and blend a collage.
• **Collage over it.** Nobody knows what is underneath.
• **Sand through the layers.** This is a fun way to make a page look vintage. It is especially great if you've collaged and painted in layers and hate it. The sanding is soothing and picking and ripping parts can look really great when you are done.
• **Tear it out** or burn part of it.
• **Cut a window** in the part you don't like. You can cut windows with a sharp craft knife placing a piece of cardboard or matboard under the page.

What if you are stuck for ideas?

Words, poems and quotes on the page I'm altering can spur me on. Look at virtual museums online or art books or magazines and collage books.

When are you finished?

This seems to be a big question. There is no answer. Every page doesn't have to be altered and larger books would take years to finish. When you feel done with a book, it's finished. Months later, I've gone back and worked in books I thought were finished.

On the other hand, some children's board books are so limited space-wise that you do not have room to do everything you'd like and you are finished before you know it.

What is the Altered Book List?

On the Internet there is a discussion group called Altered Books. It has about 900 members from 21 countries around the world. The list also has files where members post their art and links to other sites.

You can join this group by going to Yahoo and subscribing to the altered book list.
Currently, Claudette Hunter is the list mom. http://groups.yahoo.com/group/altered books

What is a Round Robin?

On the altered book list, people announce Round Robins and Serial Round Robins.
• **A round robin** is when a person sends a book around to a group of people who work in it. The book usually has a theme and sometimes the owner asks players, people who are contributing, to not work on the cover or not to use certain types of images.
• **In a Serial Round Robin,** everyone in a group sends out a book. People switch books every 2 weeks or so until all the books have made the rounds then they go back to the owners. This type of round robin sometimes has a theme, too. I'm currently involved in a collections round robin where everyone sends out a book about things they collect and people alter the book to that theme. Round Robins are great fun.

They help people see other artwork closeup, but there is always the chance of losing a book. Anyone doing a round robin should keep that in mind.

Rusted elements and aged paper bring antique charm and interesting texture to pages. Old photos and collected keys, buttons and hinges add rustic beauty.

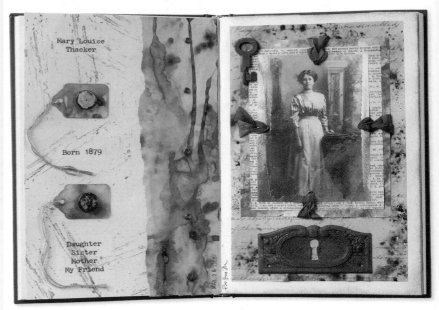

Daughter, Sister, Mother
by Roben-Marie Smith

MATERIALS: Coffee stained paper • Text printed on Clear label sheet • Marbled paper • Coffee stained letter • Dictionary paper scrap • 2 coffee stained tags • Old family photo • Date rubber stamps • Black and Brown dye ink pads • 9 Copper eyelets • 2 wood disk beads • Old key • Old key plate • Mica tile • Brown silk ribbon • Eyelet tool and hammer • Glue stick • E6000

INSTRUCTIONS: Stamp background on pages with Brown dye ink. Add eyelets to torn coffee stained paper and glue on left page. Glue tags and beads on page. Cut and place label sheet text on page. Glue coffee stained letter on right page. Place mica tile on top of photo and add 4 eyelets to hold in place. Lark's head knot ribbon in holes. Glue photo on dictionary page and marbled paper. Bring ribbon around and glue on back. Glue entire piece to letter. Glue key and key plate in place with E6000.

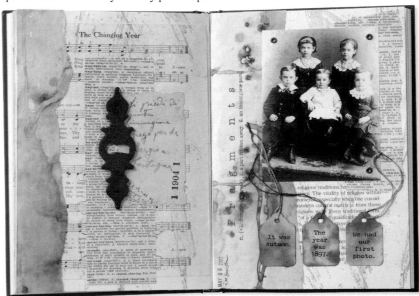

It Was Autumn
by Roben-Marie Smith

MATERIALS: Book • Coffee stained paper with printed text • 2 dictionary paper scraps • Page from old hymnal • Old handwritten note • 3 coffee stained tags with printed text • Old family photo • Date and 'Fragments' rubber stamps • Black and Butterscotch dye ink pad • 4 Copper eyelets • Old key plate • Eyelet tool and hammer • Glue stick • E6000

INSTRUCTIONS: Glue hymn on left page. Stamp background on pages with Butterscotch dye ink. Add coffee stained paper to left page. Add dictionary scrap and handwritten note. Glue old key plate with E6000. On right page, stamp 'Fragments' on coffee stained paper with dye ink. Add eyelets to old photo. Glue coffee stained paper, dictionary scrap and old photo on right page as shown. Glue tags near bottom of page. Stamp date.

Great Ideas for Altered Books & Pages

You have the book and the glue. Now, what to do? Here is a quick list of ideas from Claudette Hunter and Beth Cote

- Paint over an entire page
- Spray paint
- Rubber stamp
- Collage a picture
- Cut out pages
- Add pages
- Make marks with crayons or markers or gel pens
- Glue something to a photo
- Add 3-D items
- Highlight words with a pen
- Make up a poem using the words on the page - "found poetry"
- Mask part of the page and paint or color over the rest
- Use blow pens to stencil items
- Cut pages in half vertically or horizontally
- Old pages
- Cut out a page then reattach with jump rings
- Add an envelope to a page with a letter or tag inside
- Add a glassine envelope with confetti
- Glue on beads, puzzle pieces, buttons, dried flowers
- Sew two pages together with fibers or wire
- Sew a stick to your page
- Have an artist's page for guest artists to sign
- Fold a page over and punch holes to tie tags
- Cut out parts of a photo like a door or window
- Attach a tie or ribbon for closing the book
- Punch holes and paint behind them or glue tissue or colored Vellum over them
- Cut a diorama in many pages then glue them together or leave them unglued
- Cut out portion of the book and make a mini book
- Use mini brads to connect objects to a page
- Add fold-outs such as maps
- Line the inside covers with wrapping paper or tissue
- Use UTEE or diamond glaze over something
- Write your own text or captions
- Glue text from another book on a page
- Lace the edges of the cover with wire, plastic, fibers, ribbon or yarn... don't forget beads!
- Collage handmade papers on the cover
- Antique the cover
- Hang yarns and fibers from the spine
- Insert a card with photo corners
- Use liquid chalk or Rub 'n Buff on the pages
- Tear the book apart, reassemble in different order
- Braid thin gold wire down the page
- Cut a window and cover with lace or vellum
- Transfer copies with a chartpak marker or acetone
- Cut out the insides keeping the cover and spine, create new insides
- Make a shadow box
- Burn the edges of a page
- Apply pigment inks directly to a page

- Burn holes in the page
- Add needlework to your book
- Stipple dye-based inks on a page
- Sand away part of your picture
- Dangle beads from a cutout
- Use pastels and scratch out a picture
- Crackle the cover or a page
- Use bottle caps to spell out a word
- Use letter game tiles
- Use alphabet stamps to say oops! or anything else
- Make a pocket and enclose playing cards
- Make a pop-up
- Glue an accordion book to a page
- Brayer liquid applique over a page
- Add a poem or favorite quote
- Make a little book and hide it in a door
- Use postage stamps
- Tell a story
- Use old postcards and photos
- Make a pocket and sew the edges shut
- Used paper clay on the page and stamp a design into it for a 3-D effect
- Write a random note with magazine words
- Make your book into a treasure hunt
- Spray webbing over a page
- Glue tissue over a page
- Grommet pages together
- Color with a crayon and then paint ink over design
- Stamp, emboss and work ink into design with a cloth
- Make a page of objects you love
- Make a page in just one color
- Make a mono print on glass then print it on a page
- Make slits in book and weave with ribbon
- Make a paper weaving and glue on page
- Cut out a paper doll chain and glue inside cover
- Cut a window in the cover
- Add stickers you remove from fresh produce
- Make a journal of a day in your life and include receipts
- Glue a little writing tablet to a page
- Glue a word under a piece of glass or a flat marble
- Glue on shrink art
- Sew on buttons
- Glue pages together to make a thick block
- Use stencils
- Spread spackling over your page and carve into it
- Glue in photos of yourself as a kid
- Do cold water laminate or tape laminate with an image from a magazine
- Make a new cover out of panels of polymer clay and glue it to the old cover
- Glue an Altoid tin shrine to the cover
- Use a piece of your child's art as a basis for a collage
- Fingerpaint!!

Your Altered Book Experts

Suppliers

Most craft and variety stores carry an excellent assortment of supplies. If you need something special, ask your local store to contact the following companies.

Resources

International Society of Altered Book Artists, PO Box 56, Genoa, IL 60135
www.internationalsocietyofalteredbookartists@hotmail.com

Perfect Paper Adhesive
USArt Quest, 517-522-6225, Grass Lake, MI

Old Labels, Vintage Letters, Photos, Book Pages
Collage Joy, PMB 671, 250 H. St., Blaine, WA 98230
A Stamp in the Hand, 310-884-9700, Carson, CA
Art Impressions, 800-393-2014, Salem, OR
ArtitudeZine, ArtChix, 250-370-9985, Victoria, BC, Canada
Catslife Press, 541-902-7855, West Lake, OR
Character Constructions, itsmysite.com/catherinemoore
Dover, 516-294-7000, Mineola, NY
Hero Arts, 800-822-4376, Emeryville, CA
JudiKins, 310-515-1115, Gardena, CA
LennaLines, 860-413-9050, East Granby, CT
Limited Edition, 650-594-4242, Redwood City, CA
Magenta, 450-922-5253, Mt-Sainte-Julie, Quebec, Canada
Ma Vinci's Reliquary,
     http://crafts.dm.net/mall/reliquary
Oxford Impressions, 866-852-1602, Oxford, MS
     www.oxfordimpressions.com
Renaissance Art Stamps, 860-485-7761, Burlington, CT
Stampers Anonymous, 440-250-9112, Westlake, OH
Stamp Francisco, 415-337-5202, San Francisco, CA
Stampington & Company, 949-380-7318, Laguna Hills, CA
Stamp Studio, Inc., 208-288-0300, Meridian, ID

Lumiere Paint, Neopaque Paint
Jacquard Products, 800-442-0455, Healdsburg, CA
USArt Quest, 517-522-6225, Grass Lake, MI

Paint, Mediums, Fluid Acrylic, Glaze, Gesso
Golden Artist Colors, 800-959-6543, New Berlin, NY

Dye Ink
Ranger, 732-389-3535, Tinton Falls, NJ
Westrim, 818-998-8550, Chatsworth, CA
Clearsnap, 800-448-4862, Anacortes, WA

Modeling Paste
USArt Quest, 517-522-6225, Grass Lake, MI

Peerless Watercolors
Creative Mode, 608-224-0199, Madison, WI

Glassine Envelopes, Metal Tags
Ma Vinci's Reliquary, http://crafts.dm.net/mall/reliquary

Metallic Rub-ons
Craf-T Products, 507-235-3996, Fairmont, MN

Magic Mesh
Avant´Card, magicmesh.com

AvaSpray Paint
Design Master, 303-443-5214, Boulder, CO

Xyron Machine
Xyron, 800-793-3523, Scottsdale, AZ

Tone Pencils
Stabilo, stabilo.com

Krylon Spray Finish
Sherwin-Williams, 800-4KRYLON, Cleveland, OH

Correction Tape
3 M Company, 888-364-3577, Saint Paul, MN

Sobo Glue
Delta Technical Coatings, 800-423-4135, Whittier, CA

MANY THANKS to my friends for their cheerful help and wonderful ideas!
Kathy McMillan • Jen Tennyson • Patty Williams
Marti Wyble • Wanda J. Little • Colleen Reigh
Janie Ray • David & Donna Thomason
Altered Book Artists •
Beth Cote • Cindy Pestka • Roben-Marie Smith
Karenann Young • Claudette Hunter • Nancy Curry

Beth Cote

Beth is a professional artist who works with mixed media and book art. Her focus is altered books. She travels across the country teaching at paper arts workshops from California to Texas, at conventions and retreats. She is currently the co-president of the International Society of Altered Book Artists. Beth lives in rural Illinois with her husband and three children.

Beth's teaching schedule and altered book ideas are on her website at www.alteredbook.com
Call her at 815-335-1000 or email at cacote@aeroinc, net

Cindy Pestka

Cindy Pestka is a mixed media artist who teaches classes and is the owner of Northern Lights Designs, a web-base supplier of wonderful collage and decoupage papers. Cindy loves altered books. She has way too many found objects and thrift store treasures for her small Seattle home and loves using her collection in artistic creations.

See Cindy Pestka's collage & decoupage papers at www.northernlightsdesigns.com.
Call her at 206-353-2519 or email at pestkac@aol.com

We are our past, yet we tend to hide our ancestors in photo albums and dusty photos in our attics. Bring your past to light with this easy ancestor frame you can hang on your wall or place in an easel.

Ancestor Frame
by Beth Cote

MATERIALS: Hand shaped board book • Found objects (domino, bingo piece, old watch face, watch case, old text, old paper measuring tape) • Moss Green Cat's Eye pigment ink • Color copy of ancestor's photo • Lumiere paint • Water soluble oil pastels • Black and Brown Stabilo Tone pencil • Gesso • Matte medium • Gel medium • Matte spray sealer • Sandpaper

TIPS: Cut a niche through all pages of the book except the last page. Sand and gesso pages. Paint Copper around the niche. Rub Cat's Eye over the book and add Black tone on edges. Color random spots with Brown tone.

Apply matte medium over the book to seal pigment inks. Do not skip this step or the inks will not be stable.

Glue photo and papers on the back cover so they show in window. Glue back cover to book. Glue domino and bingo pieces inside the window. Glue words on the watch case. Glue watch case on book. Burn the edge of measuring tape (be careful). Glue tape and watch face on the cover.

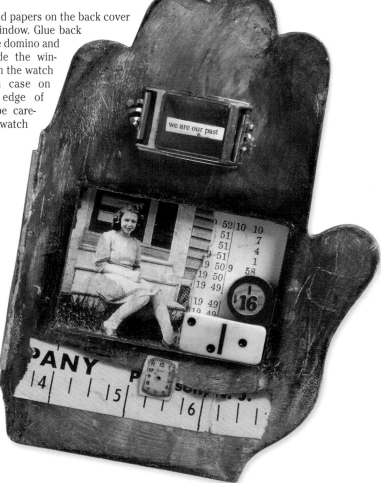